The Baptism of Holy Spirit and His Gifts

ISBN 979-8-88895-750-9 (Paper Back)
ISBN (Kindle Edition)

Book Design and Story by Don Pirozok
Editor Cheryl Pirozok

First Printing 2022
Amazon Publishing, United States

Published By: Pilgrims Progress Publishing
Spokane Valley WA. 99206
Website: www.donpirozok.com

The Baptism of Holy Spirit and His Gifts

Table of Contents

Introduction
The Day of Pentecost

In the Book of Acts is a record of the first Pentecost after the Resurrection of Jesus Christ from the dead. It is the first time the disciples of Jesus Christ are filled with the Holy Spirit. The Day of Pentecost happened fifty days after Christ was raised, "pente" meaning fifty days. Jesus Christ ascended into heaven on the fortieth day and had instructed His disciples to wait in Jerusalem until they were Baptized in the Holy Spirit ten days later.

Acts1:3-5
3 To whom also he shewed himself alive after his passion by many infallible proofs, being seen of them forty days, and speaking of the things pertaining to the kingdom of God:
4 And, being assembled together with them, commanded them that they should not depart from Jerusalem, but wait for the promise of the Father, which, saith he, ye have heard of me.
5 For John truly baptized with water; but ye shall be baptized with the Holy Ghost not many days hence.

The experience which the disciples did not yet have was the Baptism of the Holy Spirit. Jesus also called the Baptism in the Spirit the "Promise of the Father." The Holy Spirit was not yet given to the Church until after Jesus Christ was raised from the dead. The Day of

Pentecost is the Scriptural record of the coming of the Holy Spirit, the Promise of the Father who would be another comforter in place of Jesus Christ's departure into heaven. Jesus Christ said they would be "filled with the Holy Spirit," meaning Baptized in the Holy Spirit. Jesus Christ defined what the filling of the Holy Spirit would be for; "the power to be His witness." The word power in the Greek is "Dunamis" meaning a supernatural strength and ability given by the Baptism of the Holy Spirit to be the witnesses of the Lord.

Acts 1:8
8 But ye shall receive power, after that the Holy Ghost is come upon you: and ye shall be witnesses unto me both in Jerusalem, and in all Judaea, and in Samaria, and unto the uttermost part of the earth.

Christians should understand the Baptism of the Holy Spirit is the result of believing in the Lord and the power of His Salvation. The Baptism of the Holy Spirt is for those who believe and have professed Jesus Christ as the Lord. In this way the Baptism of the Holy Spirit is not the act of Salvation. Instead, is the filling of the Holy Spirit with the power to be Christ's witness. This distinction might be helpful, as salvation is the life of Christ in a new birth called eternal life. While the Baptism of the Holy Sprit is for those already with faith in Jesus Christ and is God's power in service. However, being saved by faith in Christ and being Baptized in the Holy Spirit can happen simultaneously. Also, one can also see a separation of time sometimes days or even years before a Christian already born again is then Baptized in the Holy Spirit. For example, in my life I came into saving faith and was born again with a new nature in my early twenties. I knew I had become a true disciple of Jesus Christ with a deep hunger for the Word of God. It was not until about six months later I was Baptized in the Holy Spirit and began to hear the call of God in my heart to preach the Gospel.

Outpouring of the Holy Spirit

Jesus Christ had promised another comforter after His departure, the promised Holy Spirit. Jesus Christ said of the Holy Spirit, He is the Spirit of Truth which shall indwell the believer. The Holy Spirit will act as our guide and teacher bringing to our remembrance everything which Jesus Christ has spoken. The main purpose of the Holy Spirit is to highlight Jesus Christ, as the Holy Spirit comes from the Father to testify of Jesus Christ. For the Holy Spirit does not speak of Himself, but what He hears He will speak and show it unto the saints. He glorifies the Lord, as He receives it from the Lord to show it unto you.

Notice how the Holy Spirit was sent to lead us according to all which Jesus Christ has said and done. The Holy Spirit is the Spirit of God, know as the third person of the Godhead. Not some kind of impersonal force which the Church can control and direct. Everything which the Holy Spirit does is to magnify the person of Jesus Christ in our lives. The Holy Spirit never takes away from the Lord to magnify another person. Neither will the Holy Spirit violate what Jesus Christ has already said and has been recorded in the Scriptures.

On the Day of Pentecost, the Holy Spirit was poured out upon the saints of the upper room. Peter spoke of the Holy Spirit on the Day of Pentecost as the promised Gift from God the Father. Just as Jesus Christ had promised the Holy Spirit can to fill and abide in the lives of His Church.

Peter being filled with the Holy Spirit spoke the Word of God boldly, calling for the repentance of the crowd of thousands who came to see and hear what happened with the mighty rushing wind, and the flames of fire from the Holy Spirit.

Peter called for everyone to turn from the sins and receive the Cross of Jesus Christ. Upon their repentance they should be baptized in the name of Jesus Christ for the remission of their sins. Upon receiving forgiveness of sins, they too would receive the promised gift of the Holy Spirit. Demonstrating every true believer in Jesus Christ is to be filled with the Holy Spirit. For the promised Holy Spirit has been given since the Day of Pentecost, and not retracted, but has been given to every generation of believers ever since the Day of Pentecost.

The is no junior Holy Spirit, or lesser God, as the promised Holy Spirit never changes and cannot be corrupted. The Holy Spirit was given to the Church to infill believers with power to be a witness. As one is filled with the Holy Spirit their life can never be the same. Knowing the Spirit of God has filled you and abides in you is everything Jesus Christ has promised would happen to those who put their faith in Him. A Spirit filled Church is a Church which shakes the world with a Holy Ghost boldness.

Why are so many who name the name of the Lord so weak in the testimony? Where is the promised Holy Spirit of power, Spirit of Truth, Spirit of God, filling them with the Life of Christ? Perhaps the absence of Gods Spirit in the Church indicates it is not so Holy Spirit filled. It appears the spirit of man has taken the place of leading the Church. Many Charismatics claim the power of God but deny the character of the Holy Spirit by their false doctrines and practices. Christians then end up following a man, or a movement, at the expense of being led of the Holy Spirit.

Remember when you were first filled with the Holy Spirit, and it was all about Jesus Christ then? What has happened when you compromised your first love and started to ignore the leading of the Holy Spirit. Time for the modern Church to recognize it has compromised with the Holy Spirit, and no longer carries the power or the testimony found with the Day of Pentecost. We don't need another hyped-up man-made revival; we need to surrender the Church back to being filled with the Holy Spirit once again.

Acts 2:33-39

33 Therefore being by the right hand of God exalted, and having received of the Father the promise of the Holy Ghost, he hath shed forth this, which ye now see and hear.

34 For David is not ascended into the heavens: but he saith himself, The Lord said unto my Lord, Sit thou on my right hand,

35 Until I make thy foes thy footstool.

36 Therefore let all the house of Israel know assuredly, that God hath made that same Jesus, whom ye have crucified, both Lord and Christ.

37 Now when they heard this, they were pricked in their heart, and said unto Peter and to the rest of the apostles, Men and brethren, what shall we do?

38 Then Peter said unto them, Repent, and be baptized every one of you in the name of Jesus Christ for the remission of sins, and ye shall receive the gift of the Holy Ghost.

39 For the promise is unto you, and to your children, and to all that are afar off, even as many as the Lord our God shall call.

John 14:17

17 Even the Spirit of truth; whom the world cannot receive, because it seeth him not, neither knoweth him:

but ye know him; for he dwelleth with you, and shall be in you.er

John 15:26
26 But when the Comforter is come, whom I will send unto you from the Father, even the Spirit of truth, which proceedeth from the Father, he shall testify of me:

John 16:13-16
13 Howbeit when he, the Spirit of truth, is come, he will guide you into all truth: for he shall not speak of himself; but whatsoever he shall hear, that shall he speak: and he will shew you things to come.
14 He shall glorify me: for he shall receive of mine, and shall shew it unto you.
15 All things that the Father hath are mine: therefore said I, that he shall take of mine, and shall shew it unto you.

Part I
What Happened on the Day of Pentecost?

A brake down of the Day of Pentecost is detailed in Acts chapter two. As the disciples were gathered in a room up stairs waiting in prayer for the Promise of the Father. When the Day of Pentecost had finally come the Holy Spirit came as manifestations in the form of wind and fire.

Acts
2:14

And when the day of Pentecost was fully come, they
were all with one accord in one place.
2 And suddenly there came a sound from heaven as of a
rushing mighty wind, and it filled all the house where
they were sitting.
3 And there appeared unto them cloven tongues like as
of fire, and it sat upon each of them.
4 And they were all filled with the Holy Ghost, and
began to speak with other tongues, as the Spirit gave
them utterance.

The Baptism of the Holy Spirit came first as the manifest
presence of God in the room. A sound of a mighty
rushing wind came into the upper room where the
disciples were waiting in prayer. As the room filled with
the presence of the Holy Spirit, flames of fire descended
upon the bodies of all the disciples. As the Holy Spirit
rested upon each disciple in flames of fire, they were all
filled with the Holy Spirit. The Baptism of the Holy Spirit
first came upon them before filling them with the Holy
Spirit of the inside.

What happened when the disciples were filled with the
Holy Spirit? Immediately they were able to speak in a
supper natural way called the "gift of tongues." Now the
gift of tongues is detailed in the apostle Pauls letter to
the Church at Corinth. As the result, we see the early

Church being Charismatic in doctrine and in practice. Speaking in tongues was part of the supernatural power Jesus Christ spoke of when He taught His disciples would receive power to be His witness. The tongues spoken by the Spirit filled disciples on the Day of Pentecost was heard by thousands of people who had come to Jerusalem for the Feast of Pentecost. Many different cultures and languages had come to observe the Feast from the Old Testament times. As the disciples were filled with the Spirit many languages were being spoken in tongues, by the newly baptized in the Holy Spirit disciples.

Acts 2:5-12
5 And there were dwelling at Jerusalem Jews, devout men, out of every nation under heaven.
6 Now when this was noised abroad, the multitude came together, and were confounded, because that every man heard them speak in his own
language.
7 And they were all amazed and marvelled, saying one to another, Behold, are not all these which speak Galilaeans?
8 And how hear we every man in our own tongue, wherein we were born?
9 Parthians, and Medes, and Elamites, and the dwellers in Mesopotamia, and in Judaea, and Cappadocia, in Pontus, and
Asia,

10 Phrygia, and Pamphylia, in Egypt, and in the parts of Libya about Cyrene, and strangers of Rome, Jews and proselytes,
11 Cretes and Arabians, we do hear them speak in our tongues the wonderful works of God.
12 And they were all amazed, and were in doubt, saying one to another, What meaneth this

Here is the breakdown of the tongues spoken on the Day of Pentecost. The Spirit Baptized disciples spoke in languages of other nations by the Gift of the Holy Spirit. Their speaking served as a witness to those peoples, as they heard them speak of the wonderful works of God. The Scriptures teach the "Testimony of Jesus is the Spirit of Prophecy." The gift of Tongues manifested immediately when the disciples were Baptized in the Holy Spirit. The disciples being Spirit filled spoke by inspiration of the Holy Spirit in the Gift of Tongues which could be heard as languages of other nations. Those languages spoken did not come from extensive learning and study, instead came in a supernatural way by the Holy Spirit Gift of Speaking in Tongues. One of the first evidences of being Baptized in the Holy Spirit as recorded by Scriptures is speaking in Tongues or Prophesying. In this case speaking in Tongues were being spoken prophetically as a message to those who were present from other nations. In this way Prophetic Ministry of the New Testament began with the first Spirit filled disciples setting a pattern for the rest of the Church to follow.

In several places in the Book of Acts we are given a Scriptural record of new disciples speaking in tongues or prophesying. The Lord directed the Apostle Peter to go to the Gentiles House of Cornelius. Upon Peters preaching the Gospel of Jesus Christ the Holy Spirit fell upon all those who had come to hear Peter speak. How did Peter and the rest of those Jewish disciples who had come with him know the Holy Spirit had fallen upon the Gentiles? They were all amazed when the heard them speak in Tongues and speak words of Prophecy.

Acts 10:44-48
44 While Peter yet spake these words, the Holy Ghost fell on all them which heard the word.
45 And they of the circumcision which believed were astonished, as many as came with Peter, because that on the Gentiles also was poured out the gift of the Holy Ghost.
46 For they heard them speak with tongues and magnify God. Then answered Peter,
47 Can any man forbid water, that these should not be baptized, which have received the Holy Ghost as well as we?
48 And he commanded them to be baptized in the name of the Lord. Then prayed they him to tarry certain days.

Notice the Apostle Peter compared the Gentiles speaking in tongues the same as what Peter said they had received when they had been Baptized in the Holy Spirit. Peter made no distinction between these Gentiles speaking in tongues and what the first Jewish disciples did on the Day of Pentecost. The testimony of Tongues and Prophecy was to magnify God. Did the Gentiles speak in the languages of nations, it could be? However, the Jews with Peter spoke Hebrew or Aramaic so tongues in other languages were not understood and would have sounded like foreign words. In this case we must begin to understand the distinction in Scriptures about tongues spoken which need an interpreter as they are not understood by those present. Sometimes times tongues are even spoken which are called "unknown tongues," with no know language even though spoken out loud. However, Prophecy is always spoken in a known language as spoken by inspiration of the Holy Spirit. So, on this day Tongues were not likely understood by the Jewish disciples, but prophecy would have come in understandable language which magnified God.

What happens when a Christian is filled with the Holy Spirit and speaks in unknown tongues which none who hears can understand what is being said? Over the years the gift of speaking in tongues has presented a "big problem." It has been a source of contention and division in the modern Church between those who teach the Gifts of the Holy Spirit have ceased with the canonization of Scriptures, and the passing of the original apostles. There are two divisions among modern Christians, one is called Cessationist, and the other Continuists. Another way the Gifts of the Holy Spirit can be identified by these two different groups the one who practice speaking in tongues are called the Charismatics, and those who don't called the Evangelicals. To the Charismatics speaking in tongues is an essential part of the daily prayer and testimony in the Lord. To the Evangelicals speaking in tongues is just foolish made-up gibberish. Or even worse speaking in tongues comes from an evil spirit. Later in this book we will try to sort out the issue by looking more closely at the Scriptures which validate one side or the other.

How long did the Apostle Peter say the Promise of the Father, the Baptism of the Holy Spirit would continue from one generation to the next? Peter said on the Day of Pentecost the Baptism of the Holy Spirit would continue as long as the Lord will lead men into saving faith. So even if tongues are a controversy, the Baptism of the Holy Spirit should not. If men come into eternal life, they are given the Baptism of the Holy Spirit to be a witness of Jesus Christ.

Acts2:3739
37 Now when they heard this, they were pricked in their heart, and said unto Peter and to the rest of the apostles, Men, and brethren, what shall we do?

38 Then Peter said unto them, Repent, and be baptized every one of you in the name of Jesus Christ for the remission of sins, and ye shall receive the gift of the Holy Ghost.
39 For the promise is unto you, and to your children, and to all that are afar off, even as many as the LORD our God shall call.

Here is the breakdown after Peter preached Jesus Christ, the Cross, and the Resurrection. The people who heard them speaking in tongues now we under the conviction by the Holy Spirit. They said to Peter and the rest what shall we do? Peter said, repent, and be baptized everyone of you in the name of Jesus Christ. Peter spoke of the need of repentance, and an action of faith in response to the Gospel, the need to be water baptized after repentance and saving faith. Those who repented and were baptized into Christ's saving grace would experience the remission of sins. After which they newly saved would receive the Gift of the Holy Ghost.

Peter taught the baptism of the Holy Spirit is the Promise of the Father. For the "promised Holy Spirit" was for them, and to their children, and to every generation after them until the time the Lord would stop calling men into eternal salvation. As long as this present age lasts, and the Gospel is preached men can come into saving faith and be baptized in the Holy Spirit. No matter the debate over the Gifts of the Holy Spirit, no debate should exist with men coming into Holy Spirit power to be a witness. The Charismatic experience started in the first century, which includes the testimony of Jesus the Spirit of Prophecy. In this way the gift of Tongues and Prophecy are to be understood as part of the New Testament model of Holy Spirit Ministry.

Is the Baptism of the Holy Spirit Still for Today

The question is a valid one as many teachers say the gifts of the Holy Spirit ceased after the first century Church. The controversy surrounding the "Baptism in the Holy Spirit" is not about the term itself as many teach, they are baptized in the Holy Spirit when you get saved. Instead, the argument surrounds the Charismatic version of the Baptism of the Spirit with the evidence of speaking in Tongues. The controversy is about those who speak in tongues called Charismatic Christians, and those who do not speak in tongues called Evangelicals. Today there are about 250 million Charismatics worldwide, who identify with the Charismatic experience and would embrace speaking in tongues. So, before we get embroiled in all many of controversy with those who speak in tongues and those who don't let's touch some facts.

1) Tongues is not evidence of being saved. You can be saved born again without speaking in tongues. 90 % of Charismatics would agree with this statement. Salvation

is the eternal life, while speaking in tongues is related to the gifts of the Holy Spirit. The gifts will cease to function while the New Creation life in Christ by being born again will continue.

2) The first century Church at Pentecost was Charismatic, spoke in Tongues and Prophesied. The first century Church also made mistakes with tongues and prophecy, so the apostle Paul wrote extensively on the function of tongues and prophecy. 1 Corinthians chapters 12-14 are Pauls major teachings about tongues and prophecy.

3) Paul spoke in tongues, Peter, John, and the rest of the original apostles. Peter was the first to introduce the Baptism of the Holy Spirit to the Gentiles who also spoke in tongues and prophesied. (See Acts 10)

4) Paul said he spoke in tongues more than anyone else. Paul said tongues function in private as a personal prayer language spoken to God in a mystery. No man could understand the gift of prayer when spoken as "unknown tongues." This would not make just gibberish sounds, instead an unintelligible language spoken to God in prayer. "A prayer language."

1 Corinthians 14:1-5
1 Follow
after charity, and desire spiritual gifts, but rather that ye may prophesy.

2 For he that speaketh in
an unknown tongue speaketh not unto men, but unto
God: for no man understandeth him; howbeit in the
spirit he speaketh mysteries.
3 But he that prophesieth speaketh unto
men to edification, and exhortation, and comfort.
4 He that speaketh in
an unknown tongue edifieth himself; but he
that prophesieth edifieth the church.
5 I would that ye all spake with
tongues, but rather that ye prophesied: for greater is he
that prophesieth than he that speaketh with
tongues, except he interpret, that the church may
receive edifying.

5) Paul also taught Christians should not forbid to speak
in tongues. However, its use should be done decently
and in order.
1 Corinthians 14:39-40
39 Wherefore, brethren, covet to
prophesy, and forbid not to speak with tongues.
40 Let all things be done decently and in order.

So now let's look an overview. Tongues is an unknown
language when spoken in prayer to God in a mystery.
It's function and use are best in private prayer, or in
corporate prayer meetings where it's function will not
bring confusion to those who think you are mad, out of
your mind, just babbling. However, its importance for
prayer, and at times it's public use as prophecy cannot

be understated. The foolishness of tongues has to do with its unintelligible nature, as the words are spoken as "unknown tongues." At times tongues can be spoken in an understandable language, but that seems more related to its public function as prophecy like on the day of Pentecost.

Now the only question which remains; "Is tongues still available today," and is it related to the Baptism of the Holy Spirit? I have a simple response; 250 million Christians worldwide practice the Charismatic experience. Why would the gifts of the Holy Spirit stop when the need for, healing, deliverance and salvation can still be aided by the gifts of the Holy Spirit.

Here is a challenge. No Scripture teaches the gifts of the Holy Spirit have ceased after the first century. So, what Paul taught to first century Christians about tongues and prophecy is still in force today. Paul taught you may all speak in tongues:

1 Corinthians 14:5
5 I would that ye all spake with
tongues, but rather that ye prophesied: for greater is he
that prophesieth than he that speaketh with
tongues, except he interpret, that the church may
receive edifying.

Acts 2:4-11
4 And they were all filled with
the Holy Ghost, and began to speak
with other tongues, as Spirit gave them utterance.
5 And there
were dwelling at Jerusalem Jews, devout men, out
of every nation under heaven.
6 Now when this was noised abroad, the
multitude came together, and were
confounded, because that every
man heard them speak in his own language.
7 And they
were all amazed and marvelled, saying one to another,
Behold, are not all these which speak Galilæans?
8 And how hear we every
man in our own tongue, wherein we were born?
9 Parthians, and Medes, and Elamites, and the
dwellers in Mesopotamia, and in Judæa, and
Cappadocia, in Pontus, and Asia,
10 Phrygia, and Pamphylia, in Egypt, and in the parts of
Libya about Cyrene, and strangers of
Rome, Jews and proselytes,
11 Cretes and Arabians, we do hear them speak in
our tongues the wonderful works of God.

Chapter One
The Baptism of the Holy Spirit

Why after seeing Jesus Christ raised from the dead, did
the original apostles wait in Jerusalem under the

instruction by Jesus Christ to wait and not go? You would have thought just seeing Jesus Christ coming back for the dead would be witness enough to go into all the world to proclaim Jesus Christ as Savior and Lord. However, Jesus told them to wait for the baptism of the Holy Spirit, for after they were filled with the Holy Spirit they would "have power to be witnesses for Jesus Christ." In this way Jesus Christ makes a separation between receiving eternal life through faith in Christ and receiving power to be a witness by the baptism of the Holy Spirit. For when Jesus first raised from the dead, He breathed upon His disciples saying, "receive My Spirit." After which Jesus said wait for the Holy Spirit Baptism which finally came fifty days after the resurrection of Jesus Christ. It looks like first eternal life, followed by power from the Holy Spirit. Two separate Holy Spirit experiences for two different reasons.

The Spirit of God given in eternal life comes with the profession of Jesus Christ as Lord and makes for a new creation man in Christ. What we would say when a person comes into saving faith the initial evidence of eternal life is to make a man "born again or born from above" with the incorruptible seed the life of Christ. However, the baptism of the Holy Spirit is not for eternal life as those who are filled with the Holy Spirit baptism are already believers in Jesus Christ. Instead of giving eternal life, the baptism in the Holy Spirit gives power to be a witness. As the result to be baptized in the Holy Spirit means not a work of salvation, instead those already saved receiving power for service. However, both these events can happen simultaneously with both eternal life, and the baptism of power coming together in a singular event. Also, they can be separated from each other by days, moths and even years. Sometimes a person can be saved with eternal life, forgiven, and totally accepted by God, yet they lack power to be a witness.

One the Day of Pentecost after waiting ten days the Holy Spirit came and filled those saints in Jerusalem who were waiting for the baptism of the Holy Spirit. When the day of Pentecost had fully come the Holy Spirit descended upon those saints, and they were filled with the Holy Spirit. As they were filled with the power of the Holy Spirit, the disciples began to speak in tongues in languages which they had never studied or had spoken before. This supernatural empowerment from the Holy Spirit gave them the ability to speak in the gift of tongues. In many places in the Scripture speaking in tongues is associated with being filled with the Holy Spirit. Of course, speaking in tongues is completely an unnatural way to speak, so the utterance must come from the inspiration of the Holy Spirit. Later the apostle Paul who also spoke in tongues instructed on the proper use of the gift of tongues. In this way power to be a witness coming from the Baptism of the Holy Spirit involves the gifts of the Holy Spirit like speaking in tongues. However, it is not the only evidence of power, as preaching in the power of the Holy Spirit is another aspect of the Baptism of the Holy Spirit.

So, the question comes "can a Christian be Baptized in the Holy Spirit without speaking in tongues?" The answer is yes, many do walk in the power of the Holy Spirit and do not speak in tongues, or do not want to speak in tongues. However, the argument of "saying tongues are not available today," comes from Christians who do not speak in tongues. Which is the wrong position, as the Scriptures teach the speaking in tongues as one of the gifts of the Holy Spirit. It can decrease one's own spirituality, or one's own development in the Lord comes when denying the right of Christians to speak in tongues and walk in the gifts of the Holy Spirit today.

Another false point concerning the speaking of tongues is to declare those Christians who don't speak in tongues are not really saved. Of course, this again is a false doctrine, just like those who say tongues have ceased. Both are wrong, but for distinctly different reasons. As the Holy Spirit Baptism is for power, not for salvation.

My own experience was to come into saving faith and totally being transformed by the Life of Christ coming on the inside and making me a new creation in Christ.

After six months the same Holy Spirit who led me to faith in Christ, led me into the Baptism of the Holy Spirit. When I was first filled with the Holy Spirit six months after being born again, I immediately began to speak in tongues. What was totally unique about my baptism of the Holy Spirit was I was alone at the time and was reading a book which spoke about the doctrine of being baptized in the Holy Spirit with the evidence of speaking in tongues. The only coaching and influence came from the Holy Spirit Himself as no other person was present to show me how to speak in tongues. It came purely from the Holy Spirits inspiration alone.

How To Receive the Baptism of the Holy Spirit

A. See how the Scriptures command His saints to be filled with the Holy Spirit. If God so desires to fill us with the Holy Spirit, then we can be assured its Gods will for our lives.
Ephesians 5:18-19
18 And be not drunk with wine, wherein is excess; but be filled with the Spirit.
19 Speaking to yourselves in psalms and hymns and spiritual songs, singing and making melody in your heart to the Lord.

B. Understand Gods purpose in Baptizing you in the Holy Spirit. Jesus Christ wanted His disciples to receive power to be His witnesses. Jesus said to wait until the Holy Spirit came on the Day of

Pentecost to receive the power of the Holy Spirit when being filled. If the original disciples needed to be filled with the power of the Holy Spirit even though they were eyes witnesses to the Resurrection, how much more the Christians who are almost 1800 years removed from the Day of Pentecost.

Acts 1:4-8
4 And, being assembled together with them, commanded them that they should not depart from Jerusalem, but wait for the promise of the Father, which, saith he, ye have heard of me.
5 For John truly baptized with water; but ye shall be baptized with the Holy Ghost not many days hence.
6 When they therefore were come together, they asked of him, saying, Lord, wilt thou at this time restore again the kingdom to Israel?
7 And he said unto them, it is not for you to know the times or the seasons, which the Father hath put in his own power.
8 But ye shall receive power, after that the Holy Ghost is come upon you: and ye shall be witnesses unto me both in Jerusalem, and in all Juda, and in Samaria, and unto the uttermost part of the earth.

C. Now that you see Gods command to be filled with the Holy Spirit, and the purpose of being baptized with the power of the Holy Spirit, you can now exercise your own will in faith. By asking God to baptize you in the Holy Spirit. Notice how the Church of Pentecost continued to ask God to fill them with the Holy Spirit even after the initial filling of the Holy Spirit on the Day of Pentecost. Asking God to fill you with the Spirit opens your will for God to do what He has already spoken for your life. Asking in good faith with an expectation of your petition being answered by God is essential when seeking to be filled with the Holy Spirit.

Acts 4:25-31
25 Who by the mouth of thy servant David hast said, why did the heathen rage, and the people imagine vain things?
26 The kings of the earth stood up, and the rulers were gathered together against the Lord, and against his Christ.
27 For of a truth against thy holy child Jesus, whom thou hast anointed, both Herod, and Pontius Pilate, with the Gentiles, and the people of Israel, were gathered together,
28 For to do whatsoever thy hand and thy counsel determined before to be done.
29 And now, Lord, behold their threatenings: and grant unto thy servants, that with all boldness they may speak thy word,

30 By stretching forth thine hand to heal; and that signs and wonders may be done by the name of thy holy child Jesus.
31 And when they had prayed, the place was shaken where they were assembled together; and they were all filled with the Holy Ghost, and they spake the word of God with boldness.

D. Now as you ask in prayer believing without fear, or unbelief, God will fill you with His Holy Spirit. Being filled with the Holy Spirit is not for your salvation instead it is power to minister to others. You can expect as you are filled with the Holy Spirit a desire to speak out from deep inside your belly in a supernatural way to God. On the Day of Pentecost, they spoke with tongues when first being filled with the Holy Spirit. Later the Gentiles were baptized in the Holy Spirit when apostle Peter shared the Gospel, and the Gentiles both spoke in tongues and prophesied as they were filled with the Holy Spirit.

Acts 2:1-4
1 And when the day of Pentecost was fully come, they were all with one accord in one place.
2 And suddenly there came a sound from heaven as of a rushing mighty wind, and it filled all the house where they were sitting.

3 And there appeared unto them cloven tongues like as of fire, and it sat upon each of them.
4 And they were all filled with the Holy Ghost, and began to speak with other tongues, as the Spirit gave them utterance.

Acts 10:44-48
44 While Peter yet spake these words, the Holy Ghost fell on all of them which heard the word.
45 And they of the circumcision which believed were astonished, as many as came with Peter, because that on the Gentiles also was poured out the gift of the Holy Ghost.
46 For they heard them speak with tongues and magnify God. Then answered Peter,
47 Can any man forbid water, that these should not be baptized, which have received the Holy Ghost as well as we?
48 And he commanded them to be baptized in the name of the Lord. Then prayed they him to tarry certain days.

E. Now as you ask to be filled the Holy Spirit receive the Holy Spirit by faith. Even if you do not feel anything at first just know being filled with the Holy Spirit is Gods will. As you pray and by faith receive the filling of the Holy Spirit begin to thank and praise God for His answer to your prayer. At this point you might have a desire deep inside your heart or belly to speak out to

God in the supernatural gift of tongues. As you feel this desire take a step of faith and begin to speak from your inner most being will flow living waters of the Holy Spirit. As you speak in tongues you are speaking in mysteries to God, and your natural mind might struggle with the fact you do not understand what you are saying.

1 Corinthians 14:1-4
1 Follow after charity, and desire spiritual gifts, but rather that ye may prophesy.
2 For he that speaketh in an unknown tongue speaketh not unto men, but unto God: for no   man understandeth him; howbeit in the spirit he speaketh mysteries.
3 But he that prophesieth speaketh unto men to edification, and exhortation, and comfort.   4 He that speaketh in an unknown tongue edifieth himself; but he that prophesieth edifieth the church.

Chapter Two
What It Means to Be Spirit Filled

In the book of Acts to be baptized in the Holy Sprit means to be filled with the Spirit. Which is also a command found in the Scriptures in the book of Ephesians.

Ephesians 5:18-20

18 And be not drunk with wine, wherein is excess; but b
e filled with the Spirit;
19 Speaking to yourselves in
psalms and hymns and spiritual songs, singing and maki
ng melody in your heart to the Lord;
20 Giving thanks always for all things unto God and the
Father in the name of our Lord Jesus Christ

In this way to be filled with the Holy Spirit speaks more
of a lifestyle rather than just the initial event of being
filled. Let us take in this exhortation by the apostle Paul
for a moment. Paul speaks of the influence of wine
making for merry, then compares being filled with the
Holy Spirit to a life of being influenced by Gods filling. A
Spirit filled person should be a person whose whole life
is a witness to God. All our speech should be to the
glory of God speaking in songs of praise, and hymns of
worship. Always making melody in our hearts to God.

In this way the Spirit Filled life is one of daily worship
and dedication to the Lord Jesus Christ. In every
circumstance no matter what the condition, joy can fill
the heart of the believer even in the times of trials and
testing. In all things a Spirit filled saint can give thanks to
God in all things for this is Gods will be concerning our
lives. In being filled with the Holy Spirit the joy of the
Lord is our strength as the indwelling Holy Spirit is our

guide and our comforter in every place. Even when the saints must suffer for their testimony of Jesus Christ.

Why I Speak in Tongues

Jesus Christ came in saving grace in a personal salvation when I was twenty-three years old. Many Christians were around my life praying for my salvation, I was in a room by myself when I had the Holy Spirit fill my heart with the born-again experience. I has just spoken a simple request in a time when I felt convicted of my need to surrender my life to Jesus Christ. I said out loud, "God is you are real show me." That day I became a very different person one made alive in Christ with eternal life. A newborn love and hunger for the Word of God and deep longing to know more of the Lord was the fruit of my conversion in Christ. I found out I was really looking for fulfillment all my life, and now Christ filled me with His Spirit. I wanted to tell everyone Jesus Christ was the very God of Heaven, and you could have a personal relationship with Him.

Six moths after coming into the born-again life through faith in Jesus Christ, I found myself being led into an experience which the Scriptures call the Baptism of the Holy Spirit. You must know I still did not attend a regular Church, as I had also moved into Tempe Arizona to finish my college course work in summer school. While at Tempe I found myself reading a Christian book called Power in Praise. It was about 1 AM and the room I experienced an unusual presence of God. Inside my spirit I heard these words, "go outside you are about to receive this experience." In the book I was reading about the gift of tongues which I had no knowledge. However earlier in my walk with the Lord I had heard the Holy Spirit speak these words into my consciousness, "there is more there is power." Of course, the Holy Spirit was speaking of Acts 1:8 where Jesus Christ had taught His disciples would receive power to be His witness after they were baptized in the Holy Spirit. I did not know the Scriptures neither did I know of speaking in tongues, or any who I knew who spoke in tongues. I was just hungry for all that God had for me being only six moths old in my new birth in Christ.

As I stepped outside that night in Tempe Arizona, I had little idea of what was about to happen, only that I felt strongly the leading of the Lord. Suddenly I experienced the Holy Spirit overshadowing me and being filled with the Holy Spirit at the same time. I was already given the Holy Spirit in eternal life, but this was different a fresh infilling of God the Holy Spirit, a baptism an immersion into the Holy Spirit. Upon being baptized in the Holy Spirit I immediately wanted to talk to God out of the depths of my being, only in words I had never spoken. The presence of the Holy Spirit was so real as it felt like Heaven was resting upon me. I began to speak out from deep inside of my human spirit in the gift of unknown tongues, words spoken to God not man in a mystery. Even I did not understand with my natural mind the words which were being spoken, however I knew the intimacy of communication with God was very real, deep, personnel. You must no one was present to coach me, I had no prior knowledge of speaking in tongues, neither did I know any Charismatics who spoke in tongues. I did not attend a Charismatic Church, so no human agency was involved other than the influence of the testimony which came from the book Power in Praise. I was praising God in the gift of tongues like what happened on the Day of Pentecost.

With the Baptism of the Holy Spirit came the power to be a witness for Jesus Christ. I would say one of the great benefits of the Holy Spirit Baptism is newfound boldness and ability to give witness for Jesus Christ. I began to hear the calling to preach the Gospel soon after I was baptized in the Holy Spirit. In college I had dropped out of speech class as I hated to speak in front of people. However, now I was empowered to speak to preach Jesus Christ and Him crucified and raised from the dead. The real fruit of the Holy Spirit is empowerment for the work of the Lord. Is this the main reason why Jesus Christ had the original discipline wait fifty days after the resurrection as they needed the Holy Spirit Baptism the power to be Christ witnesses.

Do you have to speak in tongues in order to be baptized in the Holy Spirit? The answer is simple many are Baptized in the Holy Spirit which refuse to speak in tongues. Are they not saved as they refuse the gift of tongues, absolutely not the greater gift is enteral life in Christ. Whereas tongues will cease when the perfect has come, referring to the Second Coming of the Lord. Eternal life on the other hand will never cease or taken away. The gifts of the Holy Spirit like speaking in tongues is only temporary to aid us in service to the Lord until His return.

Would I want to stop speaking in tongues because of the controversy which surrounds it? You must remember how it began for me giving me power for the work of service. Tongues came as a gift to supplement my service. Today as from the beginning I speak in tongues daily in private devotion to the Lord. I never knew Christians were debating tongues as having stopped after the first century Church when first being baptized in the Holy Spirit. Or even worse tongues are not really the same tongues spoken on the Day of Pentecost and are really deception from the devil. If I were in a Church Movement which denied the modern-day presence and function of tongues, would I not have a doctrinal bias against any who say tongues are for today? So being taught against tongues and manipulating the Scriptures to say tongues has ceased is taught in many Christian Movements.

I speak in tongues because of its purity of devotion, a praise worship and prayer spoken to God in a mystery. Howbeit no man understands just as the apostle Paul has instructed the Church. I want to speak in unknown tongues to God, as I had first received giving the Lord all the glory do His name. I want to desire spiritual gifts as the Scriptures instinct me to serve the Lord with all my heart, mind, soul, and being. Tongues is foolish to the natural mind as it does not come from the mind but deep inside the human spirit as a gift of the Holy Spirit has filled me. I have before spoken to other brothers in Christ who choose not to speak in tongues and have listened to all their arguments why tongues are not for today. Sadly, they reject the testimony of one who speaks in tongues and knows all the befits which come from its daily use.

1 Corinthians 14
1 Follow after charity, and desire spiritual gifts, but rather that ye may prophesy.
2 For he that speaketh in an unknown tongue speaketh not unto men, but unto God: for no man understandeth him; howbeit in the spirit he speaketh mysteries.
3 But he that prophesieth speaketh unto men to edification, and exhortation, and comfort.
4 He that speaketh in an unknown tongue edifieth himself; but he that prophesieth edifieth the church.
5 I would that ye all spake with tongues, but rather that ye prophesied: for greater is he that prophesieth than he that speaketh with tongues, except he interprets, that the church may receive edifying.
6 Now, brethren, if I come unto you speaking with tongues, what shall I profit you, except I shall speak to

you either by revelation, or by knowledge, or by prophesying, or by doctrine?

7 And even things without life giving sound, whether pipe or harp, except they give a distinction in the sounds, how shall it be known what is piped or harped?

8 For if the trumpet gives an uncertain sound, who shall prepare himself to the battle?

9 So likewise ye, except ye utter by the tongue words easy to be understood, how shall it be known what is spoken? for ye shall speak into the air.

10 There are, it may be, so many kinds of voices in the world, and none of them is without signification.

11 Therefore if I know not the meaning of the voice, I shall be unto him that speaketh a barbarian, and he that speaketh shall be a barbarian unto me.

12 Even so ye, forasmuch as ye are zealous of spiritual gifts, seek that ye may excel to the edifying of the church.

13 Wherefore let him that speaketh in an unknown tongue pray that he may interpret.

14 For if I pray in an unknown tongue, my spirit prayeth, but my understanding is unfruitful.

15 What is it then? I will pray with the spirit, and I will pray with the understanding also: I will sing with the spirit, and I will sing with the understanding also.

16 Else when thou shalt bless with the spirit, how shall he that occupieth the room of the unlearned say Amen at thy giving of thanks, seeing he understandeth not what thou sayest?

17 For thou verily givest thanks well, but the other is not edified.
18 I thank my God; I speak with tongues more than ye all:
19 Yet in the church I had rather speak five words with my understanding, that by my voice I might teach others also, than ten thousand words in an unknown tongue.
20 Brethren, be not children in understanding: howbeit in malice be ye children, but in understanding be men.
21 In the law it is written, with men of other tongues and other lips will I speak unto this people; and yet for all that will they not hear me, saith the Lord.
22 Wherefore tongues are for a sign, not to them that believe, but to them that believe not: but prophesying serveth not for them that believe not, but for them which believe.
23 If therefore the whole church be come together into one place, and all speak with tongues, and there come in those that are unlearned, or unbelievers, will they not say that ye are mad?
24 But if all prophesy, and there come in one that believeth not, or one unlearned, he is convinced of all, he is judged of all:
25 And thus are the secrets of his heart made manifest; and so, falling down on his face he will worship God, and report that God is in you of a truth.
26 How is it then, brethren? when ye come together, every one of you hath a psalm, hath a doctrine, hath a

tongue, hath a revelation, hath an interpretation. Let all things be done unto edifying.

27 If any man speak in an unknown tongue, let it be by two, or at the most by three, and that by course; and let one interpret.

28 But if there be no interpreter, let him keep silence in the church; and let him speak to himself, and to God.

29 Let the prophets speak two or three and let the other judge.

30 If any thing be revealed to another that sitteth by, let the first hold his peace.

31 For ye may all prophesy one by one, that all may learn, and all may be comforted.

32 And the spirits of the prophets are subject to the prophets.

33 For God is not the author of confusion, but of peace, as in all churches of the saints.

34 Let your women keep silence in the churches: for it is not permitted unto them to speak; but they are commanded to be under obedience, as also saith the law.

35 And if they will learn any thing, let them ask their husbands at home: for it is a shame for women to speak in the church.

36 What? came the word of God out from you? or came it unto you only?

37 If any man think himself to be a prophet, or spiritual, let him acknowledge that the things that I write unto you are the commandments of the Lord.

38 But if any man be ignorant, let him be ignorant.

39 Wherefore, brethren, covet to prophesy, and forbid not to speak with tongues.
40 Let all things be done decently and in order.

The Argument Against Speaking in Tongues

Inside modern Christianity is a debate about speaking in tongues. So prevalent is this disagreement two divisions exist in Protestantism, the Charismatics who speak in tongues and the Evangelicals who don't. I have never met Christians who speaks in tongues who says the gifts of the Holy Spirit are not for today. On the other hand, I have never met Evangelicals who do not speak in tongues who says that speaking in tongues is valid for today. There seems to be no middle road in the debate either you speak in tongues and teach the practice to others, or you don't speak in tongues and teach it has passed away after the first century Church.

Let's begin with the existence of tongues. In the Scriptures it appears tongues as a gift from the Holy Spirit did not appear until 50 days after the Resurrection of Jesus Christ. The Day is called Pentecost and is associated with the Feast of Pentecost in the Jewish Calendar. We know the first of the Jewish Feasts is called Passover and is related to the deliverance of Israel from Egyptian slavery. On that night the Blood of the Lamb was applied to the door posts of the residence of the house. When the destroyer saw the blood on the outside, he would Passover that house and all who were inside not entering into destroy the first born. Today Christians celebrates the Feast of Passover as the Cross of Jesus Christ, and the Blood of Atonement which has delivered us from the wrath of God. Even though Passover is originally a Jewish Feast its final fulfillment is found in Jesus Christ and the Cross.

These Jewish Feasts were meant to be perpetual to be observed forever. For without the shed blood of Jesus Christ no man can be saved from eternal damnation. What of the Feast of Pentecost? Is it Perpetual too. The feast of Pentecost is connected to the first fruits of the Jewish Harvest. Is the giving of the Holy Spirit the first fruits of the Christian walk of faith?
Romans 8:23
23 And not only they, but ourselves also, which have the first fruits of the Spirit, even we ourselves groan within ourselves, waiting for the adoption, to wit, the redemption of our body.

The giving of the Holy Spirit from the Day of Pentecost is just our seal the promise of God that our future redemption is guaranteed. The Holy Spirit indwelling the believers is just the first fruits of our total redemption at the Second Coming of Jesus Christ. If you want to look at modern Day Pentecost those born of the Spirit of God are the first fruits of a harvest of the souls of men.

James 1:18
18 Of his own will begat he us with the word of truth, that we should be a kind of first fruits of his creatures.

At this point just about every Christian would agree the Holy Spirit will never depart from a born-again child of God once given. The Holy Spirit indwelling the child of God is evidence of Passover they have been saved by the Blood of Jesus Christ. The indwelling Holy Spirit is also evidence of Pentecost as a child of God has the first fruits of the new creation nature given by a new birth. However, when the original disciples we filled with the Holy Spirit on the Day of Pentecost they spoke in tongues. In languages of other nations which they had never spoken before. Here is a fact speaking in tongues came with the infilling of the Holy Spirit and continued in the first century Church as recorded by Scriptures. The fact is the original Church was Charismatic and spoke in tongues as evidence of being filled with the Holy Spirit.

Christians today should agree on these points. Some Evangelicals protest and say the tongues being spoken by Charismatics today is not the same tongues as spoken on the Day of Pentecost. Some Evangelicals go even further and mock Charismatics who speak in tongues calling them "vain gibberish." Now mocking something you don't understand or don't agree with is evidence you are in the flesh, and out of the Spirit. Let's agree speaking in tongues has a component which when being spoken no man can discern the language or even understand. If you don't know the apostle Paul called this use of speaking in tongues as speaking to God and not man. This use of tongues is speaking to God in a mystery and is called "unknown tongues." No Christian can say unknown tongues has never happened and does not exist as the apostle Paul spoke of unknown tongues spoken by early Christians in the first century Church.

1 Corinthians 14:1-2
1 Follow after charity, and desire spiritual gifts, but rather that ye may prophesy.
2 For he that speaketh in an unknown tongue speaketh not unto men, but unto God: for no man understandeth him; howbeit in the spirit he speaketh mysteries.

So here are the facts the Feast of Pentecost is perpetually celebrated. The first Pentecost filled the disciples with the Holy Spirit and upon being filled spoke in tongues. The gift of the Holy Spirit called unknown tongues was taught by Paul and he forbid the Church from stopping its use. The first century Church spoke in tongues in a form of prayer and prophecy. Speaking in tongues was considered normal in the first century Church, not an act of pretense, or witchcraft, or evil spirits. It uses was daily, and the Scriptures forbid anyone stopping the use of speaking in tongues. However, the first century Charismatics would often get in the flesh and abuse the use of tongues and prophecy.

So, Paul spoke of an order and function in speaking in tongues when the Church came together.

1 Corinthians 14:37-40
37 If any man think himself to be a prophet, or spiritual, let him acknowledge that the things that I write unto you are the commandments of the Lord.
38 But if any man be ignorant, let him be ignorant.
39 Wherefore, brethren, covet to prophesy, and forbid not to speak with tongues.
40 Let all things be done decently and in order.

Now the only thing left is the argument; "have tongues continued until this day?" I offer a simple challenge. We know a true Christian has the Holy Spirit, and the Feast of Pentecost continues even today. The first century Church was Charismatic and spoke in tongues. No man can actually prove any actual time or day in history when the gift from the Holy Spirit of speaking in tongues actually ceased. An argument could easily be debated Christians in every age from Pentecost until today have had some men and women who have always spoken in tongues. Though the use of tongues and its popularity have fallen off from the first century Church, likely there has always been some Christians who spoke in unknown tongues. Today 250 million plus Christian claim the Charismatic experience. Millions of born-again sons of God speak in unknown tongues today.

Finally, no Christian can say the Bible says speaking in tongues has stopped. Instead, the Bible says speaking in tongues will continue unto the "Perfect Comes." Who or what is the Perfect? Meaning Jesus Christ and His return to earth at the Second Coming. The math is easy, we need the gifts of the Holy Spirit until that which is done in part by faith is no longer necessary. At that time what is done in part by the Holy Spirit will cease. As the saints, the children of God will see Jesus Christ face to face in a physical reality of His actual presence on earth. What was done in part is like looking by faith as in a mirror dimly will give way to the Perfect Lord at His Second Coming. Let no man twist the Scriptures to mean when the writing of the Bible was complete the "Perfect had come." And the gifts of the Holy Spirit were no longer necessary and had ceased. This false teaching twisted the Scriptures and denied the doctrine of The Holy Spirit putting personal opinions above the authority of Scriptures, and the witness of millions of Gods children who speak in tongues.

1 Corinthians 13:8-13
8 Charity never faileth: but whether there be prophecies, they shall fail; whether there be tongues, they shall cease; whether there be knowledge, it shall vanish away.
9 For we know in part, and we prophesy in part.
10 But when that which is perfect is come, then that which is in part shall be done away.

11 When I was a child, I spake as a child, I understood as a child, I thought as a child: but when I became a man, I put away childish things.
12 For now we see through a glass, darkly; but then face to face: now I know in part; but then shall I know even as also I am known.
13 And now abideth faith, hope, charity, these three; but the greatest of these is charity.

Looking At the Cessation of the Gifts of Holy Spirit

Anyone with a history with the organized Church knows there is a divide between the Evangelicals and the Charismatics. Concerning the basics of salvation and the person of Jesus Christ there is no disagreement. However, when it comes to the Gifts of the Holy Spirit Evangelicals teach the gifts have stopped with the end of the original apostles, and the canonized Scriptures. No more need for miracles as they have existed in the life of Jesus Christ, or the original apostles. Which leads to another conclusion by Evangelicals which teaches there are no modern-day apostles or prophets. So, any Charismatic who claims to be an apostle or prophet and moves in prophecy or miracles can then be automatically disqualified as in the doctrine of Evangelicalism none of this is for today. So being a modern Charismatic and having come from the prophetic part of the Charismatic Movement I would like to respond.

First of all, does the Bible teach the Gifts of the Holy Spirit are stopped after the passing of the original apostles, or the canonization of Scriptures. As Scriptures have been used by Evangelicals to teach the end of the gifts, I would like to bring out a different understanding with that main Scripture. Paul is teaching on the gifts of the Holy Spirit, and their proper use which runs from 1 Corinthians chapter 12 through chapter 14. The misuse of the gift especially tongues and prophecy are being corrected. Does the apostle Paul then teach the gifts of the Holy Spirit will then cease after the apostles are gone? Or after the Scriptures are completed? To the surprise of many Evangelicals Paul teaches the gifts of the Holy Spirit will cease when they are no longer needed. When are they no longer needed according to the apostle Paul? When the "perfect" has come, the Greek word for perfect is "Teleios" meaning of full age, complete. Now the Greek word for Scriptures is logos, and Greek word for apostle is "apostolos" meaning messenger. Neither Scriptures nor apostolic ministry are indicated in this passage as the meaning of when the perfect has come. When then will the perfect come, and what does this really teach? It simply says when we look at the Lord now being absent it's like looking at a mirror, however more darkly meaning it's difficult to see the full or perfect image of the Lord when He is away. However, when the Lord comes and perfects His work, we will see Him face to face, and the gifts of the Holy Spirit which only see in "part" will no longer be necessary.

1 Corinthians 13:8-13
8 Charity never faileth: but whether there
be prophecies, they shall fail; whether there
be tongues, they shall cease; whether there
be knowledge, it shall vanish away.
9 For we know in part, and we prophesy in part.
10 But when that which is perfect is come, then that
which is in part shall be done away.
11 When I was a child, I spake as a child, I
understood as a child,
 as a child: but when I became a man, I put
away childish things.
12 For now we see through a
glass, darkly; but then face to face: now I
know in part; but then shall I know even as also I am
known.
13 And now abideth faith, hope, charity, these three; bu
t the greatest of these is charity.

So, the Evangelical debate can never truly be based
upon when the Scriptures were canonized, as the Bible
itself teaches the gifts of the Holy Spirit are to continue
unto the Lord returns. Second it cannot be they stopped
with the original apostles as miracles have been
recorded throughout the entire Church age. Even the
Great Commission includes healing as one of the ways
to ministry in making new disciple from all the nations.
In Marks version of the Great Commission speaking in
tongues is part of this passage in making new disciples.

So, throwing out the baby with the dirty bath water is a huge mistake in Evangelical denial of the gifts of the Holy Spirit.

Mark 16:15-20
15 And he said unto them, Go ye into all the world, and preach the gospel to every creature.
16 He that believeth and is baptized shall be saved; but he that believeth not shall be damned.
17 And these signs shall follow them that believe; In my name shall they cast out devils; they shall speak with new tongues;
18 They shall take up serpents; and if they drink any deadly thing, it shall not hurt them; they shall lay hands on the sick, and they shall recover.
19 So then after the Lord had spoken unto them, he was received up into heaven, and sat on the right hand of God.
20 And they went forth, and preached every where, the Lord working with them, and confirming the word with signs following. Amen.

Do men speak and tongues today, or give prophetic words by the Holy Spirit gift of prophecy? Absolutely, are their problems with tongues and prophecy? Absolutely, the false prophetic has gained ascendency in the Charismatic Movement among those who teach prophecy upon demand, and visions, and communication with angels. Is this the type of prophecy as taught by the apostle Paul in the gifts of the Holy

Spirit. No, it's counterfeit and often soul power or even new age psychic powers. Are Evangelicals right in confronting the error of false prophecy, false prophets, and false apostles? Yes, for even in the first century Church all these things were already happening. Are Evangelicals right in the reason of identifying the false? Yes, in that is is false, and no when they teach all gifts have ceased by the first century.

Do the gifts of the Holy Spirit make me more spiritual? No, they can even make you more carnal, or a false prophet. Only when the gifts of the Holy Spirit are genuinely by the Holy Spirit do they profit the Church. Do I have a problem when someone says they speak in tongues? I should not as the Bible teaches the proper use of tongues. If I don't speak in tongues, am I not saved? The gifts of the Holy Spirit are tools for ministry, and not the evidence of a man being justified by the blood of the Lamb. Salvation and gifts of the Holy Spirit are two different areas and are not to be mixed as the evidence a man is saved or not saved.

Are there apostles and prophets today? Absolutely, however no modern-day apostle or prophet Is like the original twelve apostles of the Lamb, or like one of the prophets of Old. As those men were used of God to write the infallible Word of God and are unique in Church history. With no others to be raised up to add or subtract from what they have already written. So, no modern-day apostle or prophet can teach "new revelation", but all must submit to the written Word of God as the final authority. Are the Charismatics violating this principle by adding, or subtracting new revelations, and private interpretations to the Written Word of God? Absolutely, which makes them false apostles and false prophets. However, the false Charismatics do not void out what are true apostles and prophets which have existed in the Church from Pentecost. Even if they did not go by titles like apostle or prophet. However, in ministry calling and function have done the work of an apostle or prophet.

The Charismatics have muddied the pure work of the Holy Spirit so completely as to be easily exposed and discounted. When an Evangelical says it's a false prophecy from a false prophet, they are likely right, but may have drawn false conclusions like the gifts of the Holy Spirit are not for today, or there are no modern-day apostles and prophets. In this way you can see the confusion of Evangelicals even though they seem to have more integrity when it comes to the doctrines of the Bible. Wrong with the gifts, but right in calling our error and deception among the Charismatics.

For reason thousands of Charismatics are leaving the Charismatic Movement to find doctrinal stability among many Evangelical Churches. Even though they don't speak in tongues or practice the gifts of the Holy Spirit.

Chapter Three
Nine Gifts of the Holy Spirit

In first Corinthians chapter twelve the apostle Paul does a break down of the nine gifts of the Holy Spirit. The Scriptures which list the nine gifts are verses eight through ten.

1 Corinthians 12:8-10
[8] For to one is given by the Spirit the word of wisdom; to another the word of knowledge by the same Spirit;
[9] To another faith by the same Spirit; to another the gifts of healing by the same Spirit; [10] To another the working of miracles; to another prophecy; to another discerning of spirits; to another divers kinds of tongues; to another the interpretation of tongues:

The list of the nine gifts of the Holy Spirit in order:

1) Word of Wisdom
2) Word of Knowledge
3) Gift of Faith
4) Gifts of Healing
5) Working of Miracles
6) Gift of Prophecy
7) Discerning of Spirits
8) Divers Kinds of Tongues
9) Interpretation of Tongues

What is the meaning of the gifts of the Holy Spirit and what are some examples from the Scriptures? If we break down the nine gifts, we can see three groups of three. The are three gifts of revelation, or which show something. Those group of three are Word of Wisdom, Word of Knowledge, and Discerning of Spirits.

The next group of three are gifts which say something, or gifts of utterance, Prophecy, Diverse Kinds of Tongues, and Interpretation of Tongues. The final gifts of three are three gifts which do something, or gifts of power. The Working of Miracles, the Gifts of Healing, and the Gift of Faith.

The Word of Wisdom

In defining the set of the first three gifts, the revelatory gifts. What is the Word of Wisdom? The gifts of the Holy Spirit are supernatural manifestations which comes as ministry tools by the leading of the Holy Spirit, according to the need of the moment. In defining the Word of Wisdom, we cannot say it comes from a man's educational ability, like natural intelligence. Neither is it the wisdom which comes from God by learning the Scriptures. An uneducated man without very much knowledge of the Scriptures can have the gift of the Word of Wisdom manifest in ministering to others. As the gifts of the Holy Spirit are manifestations of the Holy Spirit given when the Holy Spirit guides.

The Word of Wisdom is a divinely given revelation which shows God's blueprint for the future. The word of wisdom reveals future events or how God plans for the future will happen. In the Old Testament many times the prophets of the Lord would speak to the future of events which God has showed them. In this case the Word of Wisdom is given as a prophecy. Another Old Testament form of the Word of Wisdom comes in the form of visions. Like what the Prophet Daniel experienced in his visions of future governments ending in the Last Day. In this way, Daniel had a revelatory experience which showed him Gods blueprint for world history and the governments of nations.

In the New Testament the Word of Wisdom can also come in the form of prophecy or visions. For example, the entire book of Revelation came in visions given to the apostle John. The Book of Revelation spoke of future events, especially related to the time of what is called the Great Tribulation. Jesus Christ spoke of these future events when He predicted the destruction of the Temple in Jerusalem. The prophetic predictions of the future Temple destruction were fulfilled in 70 AD by General Titus of Rome.

Sometimes the Word of Wisdom is shown in simple ways like thoughts into your mind. Pictures can come into your mind which then are Gods Word of Wisdom on how to resolve difficult problems, or unsolvable situations. Sometimes these pictures are given not when we are awake but asleep in our dreams. We see in the life of Joseph the husband of Mary, the father of Jesus, given warning dreams which would direct them out of danger. The point being, the Word of Wisdom is divinely revealed blueprint for the future. What God shows about the future in a revelation of the Holy Spirit.

The Holy Spirit Gift of the Word of Wisdom is like the of the Word of Knowledge, as it too is one of the revelation gifts. As the word of knowledge is part of Gods omniscient concerning present-day facts or history. The word of wisdom is also a part of Gods omniscience only revelation concerning the future. The word of wisdom can often be seen in Scriptures as prophetic predictions of the future. Or as Gods blueprint plans for future events. The word of wisdom is not natural wisdom known by thought and study. Instead, it is a gift of the Holy Spirit given by Holy Spirit manifestation.

"Does not prediction constitute prophecy?" The simple gift of prophecy contains no revelation; it is to "edification, exhortation and comfort." You ask, "Does not the Bible talk sometimes about a man prophesying when he is giving a prediction?" It does because the term prophecy can be used both specifically and in a general way. We may use terms both specifically and generally. For instance, if I said to you, "Come and have some tea," you would take that in a general sense; you would think, "He means, come and have a cup of that stimulating beverage with a little bread and butter and a slice of cake—or other food suitable for the occasion." But if you said to a grocer, "I want some tea," he would think of dried leaves in a package. Speaking specifically, "tea" is one thing; speaking generally it can be a beverage plus a whole meal. Now, prophecy can be used specifically, that is, as a simple gift to edification, exhortation or comfort, or it can be used as a general term for the manifestation of any of the spoken gifts; so that if a man is said to prophesy, he may be giving a word of wisdom—but that is using the word "prophecy" in a general sense. Oh, there is so much we could say about this word of wisdom. Remember, the Lord Jesus Christ told Peter what he was going to do, how he would deny Him. He lamented over the destruction of Jerusalem which He saw coming. God sees the future, and when He reveals to an individual what He sees and what He has determined, He gives to that person the word of wisdom. The word of wisdom is the greatest of all the gifts of the Holy Spirit. See how it can span the ages. Enoch, the seventh from Adam, prophesied (here is the word in the general sense): "The Lord cometh with ten thousand of his saints to execute judgment upon ... all that are ungodly," and so on (Jude 14, 15). The prediction has not been fulfilled yet, but we are certain the Lord is coming, and the word will be fulfilled."

Spiritual Gifts and Their Operation Anecdotal Lectures Delivered by HOWARD CARTER GOSPEL PUBLISHING

HOUSE Springfield, Missouri 02-0593
© Copyright, 1968 by the Gospel Publishing House
Springfield, Missouri 65802 ISBN 0-88243-593-0
PRINTED IN USA

The Word of Knowledge

The Holy Spirit Gift of the Word of Knowledge is very similar to the Word of Wisdom. Both gifts of the Holy Spirit are revelatory in nature which show something. However, the difference with the Word of Knowledge is the knowledge given are facts about present day realities, or history. The Word of Knowledge is never future, instead is present day or history. Words of Knowledge can also come in the forms of prophecy, visions, dreams, or even pictures to the mind. Another form which the Word of Knowledge can come in a revelation is like a single word in your intuition. A word of knowledge can be a function of the human spirit in sometimes a word is revealed to the heart before the mind can grasp it. In this way you have come to know that knowledge intuitively, by the Holy Spirits revelation into your human spirit. You know that you know deep inside, as it came by God into your heart.

Examples of the Word of Knowledge from the Old Testament also come from the Prophets. For example, the Prophet Elijah would see the events of the Kings and Generals of Syria and their battle plans against Israel. Elijah by visions would see current events which he would take and warn the King of Israel. Another example would come from the Prophet Elisha, and his servant Gehazi. After Elijah was shown how to heal the Syrian General of leprosy, Elijah refused to accept riches from the grateful General. However, Gehazi followed to ask the Syrian General of many riches but hid his greed from Elisha thinking it would not be discovered. However, Elisha saw the whole thing supernaturally which happened that very day. Elisha confronted Gehazi pronouncing God's judgment of leprosy upon Gehazi. Elisha was able to see the corruption and greed supernaturally in some visions given by God. As it was a present-day event, this was a form of a Word of Knowledge.

What are some examples of New Testament Words of Knowledge? In the Book of Acts, we see the Apostle Peter have a trance vision of a sheet of animals coming out of heaven. The Lord asked Peter to rise kill and eat those animals to which Peter replied he had never eaten unclean animals. The vision repeated three times, a vision which was showing Gods blueprint for the future evangelization of the Gentile nations. The vision was a Word of Wisdom, then followed by a Word of Knowledge.

After the vision of the sheet, the Holy Spirit spoke a Word of Knowledge to Peter about the three men sent to Peter from Cornelius. The Holy spoke into Peters heart, or even audibly aloud, either way what the Holy

Spirit spoke was a Word of Knowledge. A present-day fact of the three men's mission to bring Peter back with them to Cornelius house. "Behold, three men seek you, arise therefore and get thee down, and go with them, doubting nothing, for I have sent them." (Acts 10:19-20)

Acts 10:17-
23
[17] Now while Peter doubted in himself what this vision which he had seen should mean, behold, the men which were sent from Cornelius had made enquiry for Simon's house, and stood before the
gate,
[18] And called, and asked whether Simon, which was surnamed Peter, were lodged there.   [19] While Peter thought on the vision, the Spirit said unto him, Behold, three men seek
thee.
[20] Arise therefore, and get thee down, and go with them, doubting nothing: for I have sent them.
[21] Then Peter went down to the men which were sent unto him from Cornelius; and said, Behold, I am he whom ye seek: what is the cause wherefore ye are come?
[22] And they said, Cornelius the centurion, a just man, and one that feareth God, and of good report among all the nation of the Jews, was warned from God by an holy angel to send for thee into his house, and to hear words of thee.
[23] Then called he them in and lodged them. And on the

morrow Peter went away with them, and certain brethren from Joppa accompanied him.

"Let me remind you also of an incident in the ministry of Jesus. The woman at the well was greatly surprised when He began to talk about the life she was living. Then came the revelation about herself: "Thou hast had five husbands, and he whom thou now hast is not thy husband." Yes, the word of knowledge can expose sin.

But let me tell you what I consider to be the greatest instance of the word of knowledge in the Bible. It is in the Book of Isaiah, and these are the words: "Is there a God beside me? yea there is no God beside me" (Isaiah 45:5). There is a communication of knowledge, of God's knowledge, and before that word could be communicated to the prophet Isaiah, the entire universe had to be searched!

That is the greatest word of knowledge that I know, and now shall I tell you the smallest word of knowledge that I know? It came from a friend of mine, a man who passed on some years ago. He was a workingman, a devout man who had a large family. He bought his boy a fountain pen, and the boy went to a cricket field and lost it. He came home and told his father.

He said, "Son, take me to the field." The father knelt in a corner of the field. He prayed, "O God, where is the fountain pen?"

Here was a man who believed God knew where the fountain pen was. The Lord answered, "The fountain pen is under the tree at the other side of the field."

So, he said to his son, "Get up, your fountain pen is under that tree."

They found the fountain pen right under that tree. I call that the smallest word of knowledge I know. Between these two you can have an amazing variety of extraordinary instances that bring glory to God, inspiration to man, blessing to the church, and fear to the sinners in Zion: and cause God to he honored through the manifestation of His Spirit. Oh, let us pray for more of the Spirit of God in manifestation."

Spiritual Gifts and Their Operation pgs. 34-35 Howard Carter Copyright, 1968 by the Gospel Publishing House Springfield, Missouri 65802

The Gift of Discerning of Spirits

The final of the three gifts of revelation is the Holy Spirit Gift of Discerning of Spirits. This gift gives God's people the ability to see or hear into the realm of the unseen in discerning the unseen spirits. For example, many of the Old Testament prophets could see or hear God's angels. What could not normally be seen with natural eyes, God opened their eyes to see into the realm of spirits. Sometimes the Gift of Discerning of Spirits lets God's people see evil spirits. There are many kinds of evil spirits, and God will by His Spirit let men see the spiritual battle against fallen dark angels, or even demon spirits. One of Gods prophets was given a vision of the presence of Satan standing before God to accuse Joshua Gods High Priest. The battle in heaven was seen by Discerning of Spirits in vision form. Not only can the Gift of Discerning of Spirits discern Satan, but this gift can also help a saint discern the presence of God. As evil spirits like to imitate the presence of God, Discerning of Spirits can show the difference between what is genuinely from God, and evil spirits which are imitating the presence of God.

In the ministry of Jesus Christ, we see one of the great examples of Discerning of Spirits. In setting free the mad man of the Gadarenes Jesus Christ was able to discern the presence of dozens evil spirits which had possessed the man. The mad man came running out of the tombs speaking out loud by an evil spirit. The mad man was able to identify Jesus Christ as the Son of God and asked Jesus Christ not to torment before his time. Jesus commanded the primary evil spirit to identify himself, and he responded his name was called Legion, for they were many. Jesus Christ commanded the unclean spirit to leave the mad man. At that command, all the evil spirits began to cry out at which time Jesus Christ was able to hear them by the Discerning of Spirits. As dozens of evil spirits were speaking simultaneously, Jesus Christ heard them "in the spirit" and not in actual hearing by the means of sound waves and the ears. Hearing or seeing into the realm of spirits is the work of the Holy Spirit.

Finally with the Holy Spirit gift of Discerning of Spirits, God can give His people the ability to discern the human spirit. When a preacher or teacher has corrupted motives, but hides behind a false persona, the Discerning of Spirits can see beyond the man's pretense into his corruption. How important is Discerning of Spirits in these Last Days as evil men and imposters are waxing worse and worse, deceiving, and being deceived. This gift can save a lot of heart ache by protecting the Church from wolves in sheep's clothing.

"When a person manifests a natural talent, he receives credit for it; but when the gifts of the Holy Spirit are in manifestation, God receives the glory. This makes such a difference! I wish to speak about the gift of discerning of spirits, and the gift of prophecy. The discerning of spirits is a supernatural revelation of the unseen world. We cannot, with our natural eye, see a spirit; but if God gives to us this gift, then we can look beyond the veil and see into the realm of spirits. It does not imply the discerning of wicked spirits only; nor does it state the discerning of good spirits only; it must, therefore, mean both good and bad, whatever spirit God wishes to reveal." Carter pg. 75

The Holy Spirit Gifts of Utterance

Now we address three gifts of the Holy Spirit which say
something. These gifts require no supernatural details like
the revelatory gifts. However, other gifts often flow along
side the utterance gifts so what is being said can also have
details or future predictions. The gifts of utterance in its most
simple form does not have any supernatural facts added to it.
For example, the Gift of Prophecy in its most simple form has
no future predictions at all. Also has no present-day facts or
history like Words of Knowledge. The simple Gift of Prophecy
comes by Holy Spirit inspiration to speak to men in a simple
know language for edification, exhortation, and comfort. The
New Testament Gift of Prophecy must be tested by the
Scriptures, as the written Word of God is the only infallible
Word of God. Where the Gift of Prophecy is only spoken in
part, and a person can fall to speaking a false prophetic word.
The apostle Paul breaks down the Gift or Prophecy and its
function in the New Testament Church. Also, Paul breaks
down another utterance gift of speaking in the Diversity of
Tongues. These two gifts can create some degree of problem
by their misuse. As the gifts of Prophecy and speaking in
Tongues are some of the most controversial in the modern
organized Church, so we will take more time to sort out the
issues.

1 Corinthians 14:1-5
Follow after charity, and desire spiritual gifts, but rather
that ye may prophesy.
2 For he that speaketh in an unknown tongue speaketh
not unto men, but unto God: for no man understandeth
him; howbeit in the spirit he speaketh mysteries.

[3] But he that prophesieth speaketh unto men to edification, and exhortation, and comfort.
[4] He that speaketh in an unknown tongue edifieth himself; but he that prophesieth edifieth the church.
[5] I would that ye all spake with tongues but rather that ye prophesied: for greater is he that prophesieth than he that speaketh with tongues, except he interprets, that the church may receive edifying.

What Is a Prophetic Word?

Today in the Charismatic Movement many prophetic words are given which are completely false but are treated as authentic. Why has false prophecy grown as an epidemic inside of the Movement? First, prophecy is not fortune telling, the predicting of the future. So many modern prophetic words given to individuals are about how great their future will be, or how great their ministry will be. These types of words just pump up the flesh, and appeal to the ego. Real prophetic words are the testimony of Jesus which is the true Spirit of prophecy.

The Spirit of prophecy would confirm the Gospel, and the Cross and the greatness of Jesus Christ. Making men believe they are great, or have great calls upon their lives, or saving entire nations by great international revivals are not prophetic words. These come from "doctrinal beliefs," based upon Charismatic Theology. For example, many Charismatic prophetic types are 7 Mountain Dominion Theology teachers, teaching the Church will transform the 7 pillars of culture making for Christian cities and nations. In order to justify their doctrinal position, they use prophecy to "make a doctrinal prediction." They speak as though God was confirming their doctrine by saying God is saying, or God has shown me. However, their minds were already influenced by "false doctrine," which the Holy Spirit would "never confirm, or speak as a prophecy."

This is where the Apostolic/Prophetic Charismatic Movement has been for decades. It is no longer prophecy as defined by Scriptures. It is "using Gods name," and putting a God label on false doctrine and calling it prophecy. However, dangling the carrot of worldwide revivals has been "big money, and ministry platforms," for the well-known charismatic prophets, so they won't give up their fortune and fame anytime soon.

The gift of prophecy is spoken by the inspiration of the Holy Spirit, as a spiritual gift. It is not the pronouncing of doctrine, or the prediction of the future, or the pumping up of the flesh. In its basic use it is spoken to the Church for edification, exhortation, and comfort. The simple gift of prophecy has no future prediction, it simply encourages Christians in their walk of faith. In the simple gift supernatural revelation is not given, like a person's name, address, birth date, or any other facts like names of relatives. This keeps the fortune telling and psychic spirit under check which is being put off as prophecy in these days.

False prophets have been a problem in the Church from the very beginning. False prophets abound today in the Charismatic Movement. Why are they false? Their message is not Bible doctrine, and their prophecies are not coming from the Holy Spirit. Not every prophetic word which has facts which are accurate or is predicted and comes to pass is coming from God. Satan has his predictions too, and physic ability to counterfeit which is real prophecy. Can Charismatic Christians handle the fact many predictions which are proven true, did not come from God?

Paul teaches all Christians to walk in love when it comes to the gifts of the Holy Spirit. Christians are to desire the gifts of the Holy Spirit, and the one gift which Paul emphasizes is the Gift of Prophecy. Why is this gift of utterance so important? He who speaks in Tongues is building up himself, but he who speaks a word of prophecy edifies the Church. The simple gift of prophecy speaks to men in their known language which is clearly understood. If it is an English-speaking Church, the gift of Prophecy will be spoken in English. In comparison the gift of Tongues can be spoken in unknown languages and will need to be interpreted for the Church to be edified by its message.

The Gift of Prophecy is spoken in a known language by Holy Spirit inspiration, and speaks words of edification, exhortation, and comfort. The basic gift of Prophecy is to strengthen, build up and encourage the Church. The gift of Prophecy is not to be mistaken with preaching or teaching the Word of God. As the gift of Prophecy is inferior to the doctrines of Scripture and is not infallible like the written Word of God. The Gift or Prophecy should never replace the doctrines of Scriptures. As prophecy is to be judged and measured by the written Word of God.

Gifts of Healing and Prophecy

Sometimes the Spirit will manifest prophecy along with other gifts of the Holy Spirit. A word of prophecy can manifest words of knowledge, or words of wisdom, or even healings. Since we already have seen what prophetic words are, let us look at prophecy and healing combined. Sometimes the Holy Spirit will speak a word of healing through a prophecy, or by a prophetic dream or vision. In this way prophecy is acting like the delivery vehicle by which the healing word is spoken. The same thing can happen by a Word of Knowledge for Healing, A person may get a picture, or a word of a certain kind of sickness or disease and pronounce God wants to heal that particular person. When prophetic words of healing are spoken the Holy Spirit is manifesting two gifts however, the end result is the person is healed by the Manifestations of the Holy Spirit.

"There is another thing about prophecy: it does not improve by practice, as preaching does. The person under the unction of the Spirit can utter a prophecy as beautiful in his first utterance as any he utters throughout his life, if there is no impediment. Why? because the gifts of the Spirit of God are perfect from their inception; there is no improvement. With natural gifts, improvement is the order of the day—they are there to be improved—but not so with the supernatural gifts of God. Of course, it is possible to have an impediment—to have the channel blocked. Some do not get into wonderful liberty at first. But I have heard a person speak in prophecy for the first time as clearly and as powerfully as anyone who has been baptized twenty years.

This gift of prophecy can convict people of sin. A sinner coming into a meeting and hearing a prophecy may fall down on his face and call on the name of the Lord; he will acknowledge that God is in you of a truth. When a man is convinced that God is in the midst, it is not hard to show him the way of salvation.

Prophecy is a lovely, simple gift containing in itself no revelation, but by it all the spoken gifts can function. Let me give you a verse to show that the gift of prophecy contains no revelation. Look at 1 Corinthians 14:6. The apostle writes,

Now, brethren, if I come unto you speaking with tongues, what shall I profit you, except I shall speak to you either by revelation, or by knowledge, or by prophesying, or by doctrine?

There are two distinct contrasts here. If revelation were contained in the simple gift of prophecy, he would not have written "revelation, knowledge, prophecy or doctrine." Then we have verse three as well: "He that prophesieth speaketh unto men to edification, and exhortation, and comfort." It does not say, "to revelation." Also, let us note that when it uses the term "prophesying" it is being used in a general way and not in a specific way".
Howard Carter pgs. 72-73

The Gift of Speaking in Tongues

The first century Church was fully charismatic practicing the gifts of the Holy Spirit including the gift of speaking in tongues. A whole chapter of the Bible is given to teach on the proper use of the gift of tongues and prophecy (1 Corinthians 14), so why all the controversy of speaking in tongues today.

1) Speaking in unknown tongues no man understands what is being said, not even the speaking one.

2) The natural mind opposes what does not make sense, so tongues appear foolish to the natural mind.
3) What benefit is there in bringing fear or confusion into a Christian meeting when those in attendance think you have gone mad by speaking in unknown tongues?
4) Not every Christian speaks in tongues, for those who do not it a source of concern and contention.
5) In the past the Church has divided over the speaking of tongues; some Christians have believed its origin is demonic and not the Holy Spirit.
6) Many Christian teachers who do not speak in unknown tongues have made light, or even mocked those Christians who do speak in tongues.
7) Many Christian teachers have taught after the 1st century the use of speaking in unknown tongues has ceased with the completion of Scriptures.
8) Some Charismatics have wrongly taught unless you speak in unknown tongues you are not really saved.

The apostle Paul had a lot to say to the Church about of the gift of speaking in unknown tongues, as Paul said he spoke in tongues more than anyone else. Paul taught the gift of speaking in unknown tongues is not vain babble, instead is speaking to God in a mystery where no man understands what is spoken.

(1 Corinthians 14:2) The apostle Paul said speaking in unknown tongues is a form of prayer, spoken out of the human spirit. Therefore, Paul spoke in tongues more than anyone else as the main purpose of tongues is not public use but private prayer where no on else is present to hear. (1 Corinthians 14:14)

Verse 2:
2 For he that speaketh in
an unknown tongue speaketh not unto men, but unto God: for no man understandeth him; howbeit in the spirit he speaketh mysteries.

Verse 14:
14 For if I pray in
an unknown tongue, my spirit prayeth, but my understa nding is unfruitful.

However, there is also public speaking of tongues in a corporate gathering of Christians. When spoken in a public meeting tongue can serve as two functions. The first being as a word of prophecy spoken in unknown tongues, but then "interpreted in a known language." In this case two gifts of the Holy Spirit are required, first the gift of tongues, second the gift of interpretation of tongues. These two gifts of the Holy Spirit working together have the equivalent of a word of prophecy spoke in a known language.

The Second function of unknown tongues spoken in a corporate Church meeting, would be for prayer. Usually, the Church is praying in a known language in intercession, and tongues can also be a prayer of intercession too.

1 Corinthians 14:4-5
4 He that speaketh in an unknown tongue edifieth himself; but he that prophesieth edifieth the church.
5 I would that ye all spake with tongues, but rather that ye prophesied: for greater is he that prophesieth than he that speaketh with tongues, except he interprets, that the church may receive edifying.

If a person who does not speak tongues hears someone speak in unknown tongues without someone to interpret confusion will result and they will judge Christians as acting out of their minds. So, all the practice of the gifts of the Holy Spirit are to build one another up. Paul said he would rather speak in five understandable words to instruct, than 10,000 where the hearers have no benefit.

Finally, Paul teaches the Church to not forbid the speaking of tongues. However, this command is violated when Christians who do not practice tongues teach others it is demonic or has already passed away and

God no longer permits its use. The Bible clearly teaches the gifts of the Holy Spirit will continue until the Second Coming of the Lord, including the speaking in tongues

1 Corinthians 14:39.
39 Wherefore, brethren, covet to
prophesy, and forbid not to speak with tongues.

Has Speaking in Tongues Ceased

The argument that speaking in tongues has ceased has come from offense at tongues, and not the authority of Scriptures. The Bible does not contradict itself and has given a clear message on the Gifts of the Holy Spirit which includes speaking in "unknown tongues." Of course, Paul must address its excess and errors but, never does Paul say he did not any one to speak in tongues, or that the speaking in tongues should be stopped or forbidden. One major philosophy given by Christians who do not speak in tongues is tongues has ceased with the completion of the New Testament Scriptures. However, it is the very Scriptures themselves which teach the Gifts of the Holy Spirit will continue until the Second Coming of Jesus Christ.

Notice when the apostle Paul teaches will pass away. Paul was saying he would show a more excellent way when Christians are walking in the Gifts of the Holy Spirit. Paul said you could speak in the tongues of men and even angels, when speaking in the Gift of Tongues.

However, without love it would just be a noisy gong, or clanging cymbal. Paul then says if I have the Gift of Prophecy, or understand all mysteries (Word of Wisdom), and all Knowledge (Word of Knowledge), or have all Faith (Gift of Faith), and have not love I am nothing. Paul is correcting the abuses of the Gifts of the Holy Spirit, but never teaches stop the Gifts or forbid their use.

1 Corinthians 13:1-3
Though I speak with the tongues of men and of angels, and have not charity, I am become as sounding brass, or a tinkling cymbal.
[2] And though I have the gift of prophecy, and understand all mysteries, and all knowledge; and though I have all faith, so that I could remove mountains, and have not charity, I am nothing.
[3] And though I bestow all my goods to feed the poor, and though I give my body to be burned, and have not charity, it profiteth me nothing.

Paul does teach when the Gifts of the Holy Spirit will cease. Paul says the Gifts of the Spirit will no longer be necessary when the "Perfect has come." Now the Greek word for "perfect" is "teleios" which means completeness, full of age, man. Never is the word teleios used in connection with describing the Written Word of God. It is always used in Scriptures to describe the maturity of persons.

So here is the break down according to Scriptures when tongues and prophecy will cease. Love will never stop in this age, or the ages to come. However, where there is the Gift of Prophecy they shall stop. Or the Gift of Speaking in Tongues it shall cease, or the Word of Knowledge it shall vanish away. For we know in part (Word of Knowledge), and we Prophesy in part (Gift of Prophecy). For when the Perfect comes (Lord Jesus Christ in Second Coming), that which is done in part (Tongues and Prophecy) will be done away. When being in an immature form (child) I spoke as a child and thought as a child. A comparison to the Spiritual Gifts being immature, as compared to the maturity we have when we see Jesus Christ face to face in person at the Second Coming. When I became a man (At Second Coming) childish things are put away. Tongues and Prophecy which were done in part could only speak as if were seeing the Lord through a mirror, however dimly. For in the Gifts of the Holy Spirit we only see in part, but with the Second Coming of Jesus Christ (the Perfect) we will see Him face to face. At that time, the need for the Gifts of the Holy Spirit including Tongues and Prophecy will no longer be needed. For now, I know in part (Gifts of Spirit), but then face to face (no longer a child's way of seeing Jesus Christ) Then shall I know (the Lord openly face to face) even as I am also known. A true face to face intimate relationship with Jesus Christ in person at the Second Coming. It is at that time the Gifts of the Holy Spirit will cease.

As anyone who truly submits to the authority of Scriptures "the Perfect" is referring to the Person of the Lord Jesus Christ and His Second Coming. In no way can the perfect mean when the Scriptures are complete then the Gifts of the Holy Spirit will no longer be needed, as we have the Bible instead. This is pure twisting of the passages to justify people who are offended at speaking in tongues. Tongues and Prophecy have not ceased, even though their excess and abuse are clearly being seen today in the Charismatic Movement.

1 Corinthians 13:8-13

8 Charity never faileth: but whether there be prophecies, they shall fail; whether there be tongues, they shall cease; whether there be knowledge, it shall vanish away.   9 For we know in part, and we prophesy in part.

10 But when that which is perfect is come, then that which is in part shall be done away.

11 When I was a child, I spake as a child, I understood as a child, I thought as a child: but when I became a man, I put away childish things.

12 For now we see through a glass, darkly; but then face to face: now I know in part; but then shall I know even as also I am known.

13 And now abideth faith, hope, charity, these three; but the greatest of these is charity.

What Is the Proper Use of Speaking in Tongues?

Putting aside the debate if speaking in tongues is for today, let's see what the apostle Paul instructed the first century Church about the proper use of speaking in tongues. I will draw all my teaching from 1 Corinthians 14 where Paul teaches the Church at Corinth about the use and misuse of tongues.

1 Corinthians 14:1-2
1 Follow after charity, and desire spiritual gifts, but rather that ye may prophesy.
2 For he that speaketh in an unknown tongue speaketh not unto men, but unto God: for no man understandeth him; howbeit in the spirit he speaketh mysteries.

Paul says to follow after love and desire spiritual gifts, which include the Holy Spirit gift of speaking in tongues. Paul says one of the functions of tongues is speaking in unknown languages to God in a mystery. This kind of tongues comes with a lot of criticism by those who don't speak in tongues as they think "you are crazy, or just making up some nonsensical babble." As the words spoken make no sense to man's natural mind it is easy to make light off. However, the words being spoken come by the inspiration of the Holy Spirit and are not spoken to men but to God in a mystery.

1 Corinthians 14:3-5.
3 But he that prophesieth speaketh unto men to

edification, and exhortation, and comfort.   4 He that speaketh in an unknown tongue edifieth himself; but he that prophesieth edifieth the church.
5 I would that ye all spake with tongues, but rather that ye prophesied: for greater is he that prophesieth than he that speaketh with tongues, except he interprets, that the church may receive edifying.

Paul then distinguishes between the gift of prophecy and the gift of tongues. Paul says the basic use of unknown tongues is for self edification while the gift of prophecy is spoken for the edification of the Church as it is spoken by inspiration of the Holy Spirit in a known language. Notice how Paul wants all the Christians to speak in tongues, which flies in the face of those who want to argue speaking in tongues is not for every Christian. Also notice when tongues are interpreted by the Holy Sprit gift of the interpretation of tongues it is equal to the gift of prophecy as it can edify the Church.

1 Corinthians 14:6-12
6 Now, brethren, if I come unto you speaking with tongues, what shall I profit you, except I shall speak to you either by revelation, or by knowledge, or by prophesying, or by doctrine?
7 And even things without life giving sound, whether pipe or harp, except they give a distinction in the sounds, how shall it be known what is piped or harped?
8 For if the trumpet gives an uncertain sound, who shall prepare himself to the battle?

9 So likewise ye, except ye utter by the tongue words easy to be understood, how shall it be known what is spoken? for ye shall speak into the air.
10 There are, it may be, so many kinds of voices in the world, and none of them is without signification.
11 Therefore if I know not the meaning of the voice, I shall be unto him that speaketh a barbarian, and he that speaketh shall be a barbarian unto me.
12 Even so ye, forasmuch as ye are zealous of spiritual gifts, seek that ye may excel to the edifying of the church.

Paul then clears up a lot of confusion as Paul acknowledges speaking in tongues must have a profit and done by an order. When someone speaks in tongues it's interpretation can lead to supernatural revelations like words of knowledge, facts which could not be know through study or natural means. Paul teaches you must utter by tongues a word which can be understood, as it is spoken out in an unknown language which then must be interpreted in a simple known language. Say the Christians gathered speak English if an unknown tongue is spoken as a message of prophecy, then it must be interpreted in the English language so all present can be edified, and not just the speaker of tongues.

Interpretation of Tongues

The Holy Spirit gift of Interpretation of Tongues happen when a public message is spoken out in tongues, and no one would understand its meaning unless someone was given the gift of Interpretation. So, when tongues spoken in private happens no interpretation is needed as it is for private prayer between the speaker and God. While tongues spoken in a public setting as a message for the people present needs the gift of Interpretation so all may be edified by the message in tongues.

1 Corinthians 14:1-5
1 Follow
after charity, and desire spiritual gifts, but rather that ye may prophesy.
2 For he that speaketh in
an unknown tongue speaketh not unto men, but unto God: for no man understandeth him; howbeit in the spirit he speaketh mysteries.
3 But he that prophesieth speaketh unto
men to edification, and exhortation, and comfort.
4 He that speaketh in
an unknown tongue edifieth himself; but he that prophesieth edifieth the church.
5 I would that ye all spake with
tongues, but rather that ye prophesied: for greater is he that prophesieth than he that speaketh with tongues, except he interpret, that the church may receive edifying.

"Different aspects of speaking in tongues appear in Acts and 1 Corinthians, such that the Assemblies of God declare that the gift in Acts "is the same in essence as the gift of tongues" in 1 Corinthians "but different in purpose and use".[46] They distinguish between (private) speech in tongues when receiving the gift of the Spirit, and (public) speech in tongues for the benefit of the church. Others assert that the gift in Acts was "not a different phenomenon" but the same gift being displayed under varying circumstances.[48] The same description—"speaking in tongues"—is used in both Acts and 1 Corinthians, and in both cases the speech is in an unlearned language.

The New Testament describes tongues largely as speech addressed to God, but also as something that can potentially be interpreted into human language, thereby "edifying the hearers" (1 Cor 14:5, 13). At Pentecost and Caesarea the speakers were praising God (Acts 2:11; 10:46). Paul referred to praying, singing praise, and giving thanks in tongues (1 Cor 14:14–17), as well as to the interpretation of tongues (1 Cor 14:5), and instructed those speaking in tongues to pray for the ability to interpret their tongues so that others could understand them (1 Cor 14:13). While some people limit speaking in tongues to speech addressed to God— "prayer or praise",[42] others claim that speaking in tongues be the revelation from God to the church, and when interpreted into human language by those imbued with the gift of interpretation of tongues for the benefit of others present, may be considered equivalent to prophecy.[49]

Music. Musical interludes of glossolalia are sometimes described as singing in the Spirit. Some hold that singing in the Spirit is identified with singing in tongues in 1 Corinthians 14:13–19,[50][51] which they hold to be "spiritual or spirited singing", as opposed to "communicative or impactive singing" which Paul refers to as "singing with the understanding".[52]

Sign for unbelievers (1 Cor 14:22). Some assume that tongues are "a sign for unbelievers that they might believe",[53] and so advocate it as a means of evangelism. Others point out that Paul quotes Isaiah to show that "when God speaks to people in language they cannot understand, it is quite evidently a sign of God's judgment"; so if unbelievers are baffled by a church service they cannot understand because tongues are spoken without being interpreted, that is a "sign of God's attitude", "a sign of judgment".[54] Some identify the tongues in Acts 2 as the primary example of tongues as signs for unbelievers

Comprehension. Some say that speaking in tongues was "not understood by the speaker".[42] Others assert that "the tongues-speaker normally understood his own foreign-language message".[55] This last comment seems to have been made by someone confusing the "gift of tongues" with the "gift of the interpretation of tongues" , which is specified as a different gift in the New Testament, but one that can be given to a person who also has the gift of tongues. In that case, a person understands a message in tongues that he has previously spoken in an unknown language." (Article of Wikipedia)

"Let me add just a little about the gift of interpretation. People have wondered about it. They have asked me, "Brother Carter, how does the gift of interpretation come?" Well, I will give a personal experience. When I first began to interpret, I saw everything in the most graphic way; the Lord was pleased to give me a picture, and all I had to do was to describe it in the Spirit. Then that passed away, and I had interpretation by words. Words would come and I would just speak them out. Later came the most difficult time of all, which I am experiencing at the present time. When a message in tongues is ended, I generally have nothing in my mind at all; I have to step out in the dark, as it were; or, to use a Bible figure, I have to start out in faith like Abraham, not knowing whither I am going. This gift of interpretation is a complementary gift to the speaking with other tongues. Without it a person should not speak publicly in tongues, if there is no interpreter present. He may speak once, but if no interpretation is given, he should not speak a second time. Better still, let him pray that he might interpret the message himself.

Interpretations should not be given in a strained way. I knew a young man who used to twist and struggle greatly before he gave an interpretation; it seemed to be a painful experience for him.

The same thing happened in my church in London. There was a lady who had a good gift of interpretation, so we left the ministry of interpretation to her. However, she developed an idiosyncrasy that was very distressing. Members of the congregation asked me if I would speak to her about it. They were distressed about the scream that usually preceded the interpretation. I said to the sister one day, "Just come with me for one moment," and I took her away from the congregation so that I could talk with her privately. I said, "I want to speak to you about your gift of interpretation." She froze stiff, anticipating what was coming—and that didn't help me, because I always found it difficult to say anything along the line of correction to a lady. But I had to go through with it, even though the atmosphere was so antagonistic. I thought: "How can I tell her about this scream without offending her?" Then a happy thought came. I said, "Sister, what I want to say can be expressed very briefly. It is this: we want the train to start without the whistle blowing."

It was the shriek of the whistle that got on our nerves. For about three weeks after this we had no interpretations. Then the dear sister got over it and began to interpret again, and there was no struggle, no scream, but beautiful interpretations—the train without the whistle.

It is wonderful to have a message in tongues with interpretation—not that all messages are striking and remarkable, but the fact that God is in manifestation in the Church is so encouraging. It is an assurance to us that we are in the line of His will, and that we have no need to write Ichabod over our meetings. I trust that we shall never lose the manifestations of the Spirit of God from our Pentecostal churches."
Howard Carter pgs. 92-95

The Power Gifts

We now turn our attention to the three gifts of power: the gift of healings, the gift of working of miracles, and the gift of faith. These three gifts demonstrate the power of God which defy the natural laws of nature. So, in their very essence these gifts of the Holy Spirit draw a lot of attention as they openly display the supernatural acts of God.

The Gift of Healings

One of the main aspects of ministry in both the Old and New Testaments is God power to heal all manner of sickness and diseases. One of the main ways Jesus Christ demonstrated His compassion was by healing the sick, cleansing the leprosy, and even raising the dead. Jesus

Christ also commissioned His disciples to heal the sick as they preached the Gospel of the Kingdom. With the Day of Pentecost, the Holy Spirit was poured out for the Church of the redeemed. Right away we see new Christians disciples displaying the Holy Spirit power to heal the sick. Just as it was with the original disciples, now the new disciples were able to heal the sick.

The Bible demonstrates there are many ways in which God heals the Sick. However, one of the ways God heals through the disciples of every part of the Church age is the gift of the Holy Spirit of Healings. Notice the Scriptures speak of multiple types of healings from the the gifts of healing. Which means one Christian may have one type of healing for certain sickness or diseases, while another has a different type of healing. While the operations and administrations of these healing gifts is given to each one by the Holy Spirit.

1 Corinthians 14:9
9 To another faith by the same Spirit; to another the gifts of healing by the same Spirit;

"Let us turn for our reading to 1 Corinthians 14:1-6, and then to 12:9: "To another faith by the same Spirit; to another the gifts of healing by the same Spirit." This evening we are going to consider gifts of healing. God delights to heal His people. During the forty years that the children of Israel were marching across the desert, there was not one feeble person in all their tribes. God can keep us all well; isn't that a pleasant thought! We can be well and strong in the Lord! Gifts of healing—notice, please, that it is a composite gift; it does not say "gift" of healing, but "gifts." Although it is one manifestation, it is a composite manifestation, even as a bunch of grapes is not one grape, but a cluster of many grapes; so, with gifts of healing, there are many gifts all clustered together in the one composite manifestation. One might ask, "How many gifts are there?" Where the Bible is silent it is a very good thing to remain silent, and not to speak when the Bible doesn't speak, or to speak only as far as the Bible does. I will go only as far as I find light in God's Word. How many gifts, we are asked, are there in this manifestation? In the New Jerusalem there will be the tree of life, and it says that on the tree of life there are twelve different kinds of fruit. Every fruit will have its own leaf, so there will be twelve different kinds of leaves. It says that the leaves of the tree are for the healing of the nations; so, it may be there are twelve gifts of healing; such is my inference. Why twelve? Because it would be possible to classify all the diseases to which human nature is heir under twelve headings, in twelve categories; and if that is so, then God has covered every category of disease

Carter pg. 48 Spiritual Gifts and Their Operation

Praying for Healing and the Gift of Healing

It is the privilege of every believer to pray and ask for healing and to receive answers from God to his prayer.

The Bible says, "Is anyone among you sick? Let him call for the elders of the church, and let them pray over him, anointing him with oil in the name of the Lord. And the prayer of faith will save the sick, and the Lord will raise him up. And if he has committed sins, he will be forgiven" (James 2:5).

However, praying for healing should be distinguished from the "gift of healing" (1 Corinthians 12:7) which the Lord distributes "to each one individually as He wills" (1 Corinthians 12:11). This gift was given by divine direction and granted healing to specific people for specific purposes. For the Lord knows the capacities and the needs existing in the experience of each individual and He does that which is best.

A Sick Healing Eschatology

The push to make the supernatural proof of a better "end times view," has brought a lot of Charismatics into philosophical assumptions which violate the Word of God. First of all, healing is related to this age before the resurrection of the righteous, a temporary means to provide for our mortal bodies. Upon the resurrection of the righteous, the body becomes immortal and glorified and can die no more. Healing is just temporal and cannot deliver Christians or anyone else from their mortality. Healing was never meant to build an eternal salvation upon instead the Cross of Jesus Christ with forgiveness of sins, and eternal life are all included in "eternal salvation." Healing "cannot provide eternal salvation and is destined to pass away giving way to immorality and eternal judgment. Healing is not the evidence a man is shaved, neither is it the evidence a man will "enter the kingdom of heaven."

It is abundantly clear Jesus Christ warned not everyone who can demonstrate miracles, prophecy, or even cast out evil spirits will "be allowed to enter the kingdom of heaven." A man can be healed, and still die in his sins, and go to Hell Fire being judged at the Great White Throne to the Lake of Fire for all eternity. On the other hand, a man can die sick with sores all over his body suffering greatly in this life, and upon death go in Paradise. The difference being, the man had been forgiven of his sins through the Cross, and commitment to the Lordship of Jesus Christ. To build an eschatology upon healing, miracles, signs and wonders, or even prophecy is to deal with powers which are destined to "pass away." However, the Kingdom of heaven, the forgiveness of sin, and eternal life by faith in Jesus Christ is eternal. A Biblical eschatology must be built on a clear Second Coming, the Cross of Jesus Christ, the resurrection of Jesus Christ, the Judgment of both the righteous and unrighteous at the Second Coming, and the resurrection of the dead. Healing is not part of the equation which determines eternal judgment, and man's position for all eternity.

Do you know even the greatest healing ever demonstrated is no guarantee of eternal salvation? Did you know even hundreds of healings in a healing meeting is no guarantee of eternal salvation? Let's consider the resurrection of Lazarus from the dead, after four days being dead. This one of the great sings Jesus Christ gave as proof of His divinity, His power over sin and death. Lazarus body had already begun to decay when Jesus Christ called him forth from among the dead back into Lazarus' body. A great display of power, a great sign, tremendous authority. However, the body which Lazarus was raised back into was a "mortal body," so with age Lazarus would die again. Once again healing is proven to be temporal based upon sickness and disease. It is also one of the great proofs "we are not yet" in the kingdom age, as sickness disease, and death are still present. As the kingdom saints are "all resurrected and can die no more." As healing is not the "fullness of salvation," instead resurrection is that evidence.

So, with eschatology the Kingdom of heaven, and the Kingdom age relates to the resurrection of the dead, which is based upon eternal salvation, not temporal healing. Now let's consider these sayings, "healing is just a taste of the power of the age to come." Did you get that? The glorified saints walk in the fulness of power being immortal, having power over death and cannot be made sick or weakened by sin and death. This is not "possible in this age?" Next when do the sons of

God appear? The Bible is clear, we do not yet know what we shall be, but when Jesus Christ appears we will be like Him. It requires our resurrection to be like Christ, as sin and death still limit the expression of our sonship. When the sons of God appear in the resurrection the Scriptures confirm is the time of our glorification, and not before.

Not let's take on a Charismatic Sacred Cow. "Truly, Truly I say to you the works I do you shall do also, and even greater works than these..." John 14:12 The signs and wonders Charismatics like to quote this verse, saying that we are "just like Jesus." However, it is simply clear no Christian has "ever displayed the authority Jesus Christ walked in." First Christians have the "Spirit by measure," in other words Charismatic's are always "seeking the anointing," so they can gain power translating into the ability to do more miracles. They are "anointed by measure," while Jesus Christ has "unlimited anointing." The problem being two-fold 1) Jesus Christ is God, 2) Jesus Christ had a sinless life. No man could take His life, instead he must freely "lay it down." Jesus Christ was not a man born in sin with a sin nature. In comparison we were born with a sin nature having many sins are weakened by the flesh, and only have the anointing by measure.

However, in the next age when the saints become immortal and glorified, they will at that time "do the greater works" which Jesus Christ was teaching. As the immortal saints will at that time rule the nations with Jesus Christ, with a rod or iron and can die no more. Putting all "your eschatology," in this age makes for a fantasy world of the supernatural. Many Charismatics simply are building in this age what is not humanly possible. Instead, they experience some healing miracles and then attempt to build a whole kingdom of heaven on earth eschatology around it. It's a fraud and sham, it's just healing, not the eternal kingdom. As these same apostles cannot even stop their own morality. With time and age, will die like mere mortals, and not like "gods."

Notice verse 50; "flesh and blood cannot inherit the kingdom of heaven..." must be raised into an immortal body before you can inherit.

1 Corinthians 15:50-58
50 Now this I say, brethren, that flesh and blood cannot inherit the kingdom of God; neither doth corruption inherit incorruption.
51 Behold, I shew you a mystery; We shall not all sleep, but we shall all be changed,
52 In a moment, in the twinkling of an eye, at the last trump: for the trumpet shall sound, and the dead shall be raised incorruptible, and we shall be changed.
53 For this corruptible must put on incorruption, and this mortal must put on immortality.
54 So when this corruptible shall have put on incorruption, and this mortal shall have put on

immortality, then shall be brought to pass the saying that is written, Death is swallowed up in victory.

55 O death, where is thy sting? O grave, where is thy victory?

56 The sting of death is sin; and the strength of sin is the law.

57 But thanks be to God, which giveth us the victory through our Lord Jesus Christ.

58 Therefore, my beloved brethren, be ye steadfast, unmoveable, always abounding in the work of the Lord, forasmuch as ye know that your labour is not in vain in the Lord.

Working of Miracles

The gift that we are considering is mentioned in 1 Corinthians 12:10: "To another the working of miracles." This is a spectacular gift, full of signs and wonders: a gift that was more in evidence in the Old Testament than in the New. In the New Testament God was showing His compassion; in the Old Testament He was demonstrating His power. Some people have erroneously supposed that the power of God is demonstrated only in the conversion of souls. It goes without saying that the conversion of a soul is a supernatural experience; it is indeed a miracle. A person does not become converted by turning over a new leaf or living a better life; he is converted when the power of God gives him new life. The working of miracles, however, is a supernatural manifestation of the power of God that alters, suspends, or in some other way controls the laws of nature.

Howard Carter pg. 59

The gift of miracles is a genuine spiritual gift that the Lord gave to the church. It is the supernatural ability to perform special signs that testify to the truth of the message of Jesus Christ. There are a number of important observations that need to be made about this spiritual gift. First, the miracle-worker was able to do things which were plainly supernatural. Indeed, there is no natural explanation for the deeds which they did. Like the gifts of healing, this spiritual gift is spoken of in the plural. This may refer to various types of miracles working gifts. The many miracles that Jesus' disciples performed after His ascension into heaven fulfills a prediction which He made. Indeed, the Lord promised that they would do greater miracles that He did. With a number of disciples performing miracles this came to pass. While miracles were performed by some believers in the early church this was not true of every believer. Neither do we find miracles recorded in every place in which the disciples ministered. The Apostle Paul was one who had this gift. Furthermore, there were some unusual miraculous gifts which were attributed to him. It is debated among Christians as to whether this gift still exists in the church. Some limit the gift of miracles to the apostles. When they died out the ability to perform miracles died with them. Those who argue against this viewpoint point out that some people who were non-apostles, such as Stephen, also worked miracles. Therefore, they were not limited to the apostles. If someone claims to have the gift of miracles, then they should be able to duplicate similar miracles to what we find in the New Testament.

Here are some examples of the working of miracles.

2 Kings 4:1-7
1 Now there cried a certain woman of the wives of the sons of the prophets unto Elisha, saying, Thy servant my husband is dead; and thou knowest that thy servant did fear the Lord: and the creditor is come to take unto him my two sons to be bondmen.
2 And Elisha said unto her, What shall I do for thee? tell me, what hast thou in the house? And she said, Thine handmaid hath not any thing in the house, save a pot of oil.
3 Then he said, Go, borrow thee vessels abroad of all thy neighbours, even empty vessels; borrow not a few.
4 And when thou art come in, thou shalt shut the door upon thee and upon thy sons, and shalt pour out into all those vessels, and thou shalt set aside that which is full.
5 So she went from him, and shut the door upon her and upon her sons, who brought the vessels to her; and she poured out.
6 And it came to pass, when the vessels were full, that she said unto her son, Bring me yet a vessel. And he

said unto her, There is not a vessel more. And the
oil stayed.
7 Then she came and told the man of God. And he
said, Go, sell the oil, and pay thy debt, live thou of the
rest.

Acts 3:1-7

1 Now Peter and John went up together into the
temple at the hour of prayer, being the ninth hour.
2 And a certain man lame from his mother's womb was
carried, whom they laid daily at the gate of the
temple which is called Beautiful, to
ask alms of them that entered into the temple;
3 Who seeing Peter and John about to go into the
temple asked an alms.
4 And Peter, fastening his
eyes upon him with John, said, Look on us.
5 And he gave heed unto them, expecting to
receive something of them.
6 Then Peter said, Silver and gold have I none; but such
as I have give I thee: In the name of JesusChrist of
Nazareth rise up and walk.
7 And he took him by the
right hand, and lifted him up: and immediately his feet a
nd bones received.
8 And he leaping
up stood, and walked, and entered with them into the
temple, walking, and leaping, and praising God.
9 And all the people saw him walking and praising God:

Looking For Miracles or Looking for Jesus Christ

In most religions of the world the practice is with images of wood, or stone, which repent the gods being worshipped. For those who don't follow idol images, superstitions are practiced like curses, or practices which release supernatural favor or blessing. For those who follow supernatural powers like the New Age Movement the person becomes the "god like being," with spiritual power and ability. Looking for the supernatural is common to all humanity, a belief in God like powers.

What happens with Christians when it becomes the pursuit of supernatural experiences? Does the Bible teach Christians to seek the supernatural? Probably, one of the greatest deceptions inside the Charismatic Movement is to seek a power encounter, a spiritual feeling, or spiritual high, a mood-altering encounter from the "realm of the spirit." All this pursuit is done under the banner of the Kingdom of Heaven on earth, or signs and wonders, or the Presence, or the anointing. All this is to mean Christians are hosting the presence of God, or the manifest presence of the Holy Spirit.

Jesus Christ performed miracles, one of the great demonstrations which proved He was the prophet which was greater than Moses was the multiplication of food in the wilderness. After the great sign of feeding the multitude of the wilderness Jesus had to rebuke the crowd which followed Him for the signs and wonders.

John 6:26-30
26 Jesus answered them and said, Verily, verily, I say unto you, Ye seek me, not because ye saw the miracles, but because ye did eat of the loaves, and were filled.
27 Labour not for the meat which perisheth, but for that meat which endureth unto everlasting life, which the Son of man shall give unto you: for him hath God the Father sealed.
28 Then said they unto him, what shall we do, that we might work the works of God?
29 Jesus answered and said unto them, this is the work of God, that ye believe on him whom he hath sent.
 30 They said therefore unto him, what sign shewest thou then, that we may see, and believe thee? what dost thou work?

The Jews require a sign, or they simply will not believe. However, are Christians to seek signs and wonders, or are we to seek the person of Jesus Christ? Will signs and wonders transform the world by the power of the Holy Spirit? Will transforming atmospheres so people can "feel God," make for heaven on earth? This may be surprising to many Charismatics we are not to seek supernatural encounters. Instead, the person of Jesus Christ is whom we are instructed to follow. The power of a Spirit filled life comes from laying our lives down and picking up the Cross in self denial.

Even the power we receive from the Holy Spirit is the power to be a witness. The actual Greek word for witness is "martos," in English means martyr. The witness of a Spirit filled life; a Baptism of the Holy Spirit is the power of God to live as a living sacrifice. To deny yourself and follow the Lord in a life of surrender. Do Christians realize you can prophesy, pray for miracles, or healing, and still not have a surrendered life to Christ? It may be the single most deceptive issue in the signs and wonders Movement. The issue looks like "power seekers, wanting the supernatural," without a personal loss or cost. It has led to New Age magic being practiced, as prophecy, fortune telling, magical experiences, signs, mystical feelings are now being labeled the work of the Holy Spirit. All this can be experienced without Jesus Christ and without the Cross.

Real power from the Holy Spirit comes from consecrated lives in complete surrender to Jesus Christ. Following the Lord by picking up the Cross as a living sacrifice and seeking to be crucified with Christ. Preaching the message of the Cross, so the Holy Spirit can glorify Jesus Christ. The Holy Spirit will confirm the preaching of the Gospel with authentic signs wonders and miracles which will lead men to faith in Jesus Christ. The signs and wonders of the Holy Spirit confirm the Gospel, and the glorification of Jesus Christ. All other displays of power which don't reveal Jesus Christ, are simply strange magic.

The Gift of Faith
The gift of faith can be defined as faith imparted by the Spirit of God for protection in times of danger, or for divine provision, or it may include the ability to impart blessing.
Carter pg. 44

An Angel Frees Peter

In this case we see the Church in prayer, and Peter walking in faith for deliverance. The fact Peter was told he would be older before his death by Jesus Christ in a prophetic word kept Peter in the position of waiting for his freedom from prison. The gift of faith was working with Peter in the face of his own martyrdom. Peter trusted the Lord and God sent His Angel to protect Peter from danger and harm.

Acts 12:5-11
5 Peter therefore was
kept in prison: but prayer was made without
ceasing of the church unto God for him.
6 And when Herod would have brought him forth, the
same night Peter was sleeping between two
soldiers, bound with two chains: and the
keepers before the door kept the prison.
7 And, behold, the angel of the Lord came
upon him, and a light shined in the prison: and he
smotePeter on the side, and
raised him up, saying, Arise up quickly. And his chains fel

I off from his hands.
8 And the angel said unto him, Gird thyself, and bind
on thy sandals. And so he did. And he saith unto
him, Cast thy garment about thee, and follow me.
9 And he went out, and
followed him; and wist not that it was true which was
done by the angel; but thought he saw a vision.
10 When they were past the first and the
second ward, they came unto the iron gate that
leadeth unto the city; which opened to them of his own
accord: and they went out, and passed on
through one street; and forthwith the
angel departed from him.
11 And when Peter was come to himself, he said, Now I
know of a surety, that the Lord hath sent his
angel, and hath delivered me out of the hand of
Herod, and from all the expectation of the people of the
Jews.

"Faith is a gift that enables one to believe for God to
undertake in a supernatural way. Daniel was thrown
into the lions' den because he would not cease praying
to his God. There was the test. He must either stop
praying or be cast into the lions' den. (Some people stop
praying without any threat of a lions' den awaiting
them.) Daniel opened his window toward the east and
prayed to his God. As a result, he was committed to the
den of lions. What did Daniel do in the den? He did
nothing! At least nothing that was evident; but God had

given him faith, faith so mighty that the lions could not touch him.

There was protection from danger. You ask, "How does this gift differ from the working of miracles?" That is a good question, and we must endeavor to answer it. You remember that Samson, when he was going down to make arrangements for his marriage to a Philistine young woman, was met by a lion. What did Samson do when the beast sprang at him? The Spirit of the Lord came mightily upon him, and he tore the lion as if it had been a goat; he flung its carcass by the wayside and went on his journey. That was a miracle; that was the working of miracles in contradistinction to the experience of Daniel who did not touch a beast in the lions' den. If they had put Samson in the lions' den, he might have cracked all their jaws as soon as possible, and then lain down to rest on one of the carcasses until they let him out in the morning. Daniel and Elijah did nothing but trust. It was that mighty sustained faith that brought into operation the powers of the world to come. With Daniel, God sent His angel and stopped the lions' months. That is the gift of faith—God doing the work for you. The working of miracles is God doing the work through you" Carter pg. 39

"The Gift of Special Faith
In previous chapters, we covered the revelation gifts of the Holy Spirit: the word of wisdom, the word of knowledge, and the discerning of spirits.

Now let's study the three power gifts of the Holy Spirit: the gift of faith, the working of miracles, and the gifts of healings.

In this lesson, we will discuss the first of the power gifts: the gift of faith. The Amplified Bible reads, "To another (wonder-working), faith . . ." (1 Cor. 12:9). This gift of the Spirit is also called special faith.

The Gift of Special Faith Is Not the Same as Saving Faith

Every believer already has general faith or saving faith, which is also a gift. Ephesians 2:8 says, "For by grace are ye saved through faith; and that not of yourselves: it is the gift of God."

The faith that you are saved by is a gift of God, but it is not one of the nine gifts of the Spirit. Saving faith is given to you through hearing the Word, because the Bible says, "So then faith saving faith] cometh by hearing, and hearing by the word of God" (Rom. 10:17).

The faith which we are talking about in this lesson — special faith — is something other than general faith or saving faith. It is a supernatural manifestation of the Holy Spirit whereby a believer is empowered with special faith, or wonder-working faith, and it is beyond simple saving faith.

The gift of faith is the greatest of the three power gifts. And this gift is miraculous just as the rest of the gifts of the Spirit are miraculous.

The gift of faith is a gift of the Spirit to the believer in order that he might receive miracles. The working of miracles, on the other hand, is a gift of the Spirit given to the believer that he might work miracles. One gift receives, the other does something. Notice the Bible says, "To another the WORKING of miracles . . ." (1 Cor. 12:10). In other words, when you receive a miracle, you don't work the miracle. But when you perform a miracle by the unction of the Holy Ghost, you are working a miracle by this supernatural gift of the Spirit, the working of miracles.

These power gifts are very closely associated one with another and many times work together. The same is true of the revelation gifts; they also are closely related, and work together as do the utterance gifts. It is also important to note that all of the gifts of the Spirit operate by faith — by ordinary faith on the part of the believer through which the gift is being manifested. In other words, a person must step out in faith and yield to the promptings of the Holy Spirit. That's where simple faith is involved. This ordinary faith is the faith that comes by hearing God's Word. Therefore, the gifts of the Spirit do not operate by the gift of faith, but they do operate by general or ordinary faith. Remember, the Bible says, ". . . If thou canst believe, all things are possible to him that believeth" (Mark 9:23).

As we said, the gift of faith, one of the nine gifts of the Spirit, is separate and distinct from the simple gift of saving faith. The gift of faith — special faith — is also distinct from the faith that is a fruit of the Spirit (Gal. 5:22). We read about the fruit of the Spirit, one of which is faith, in Galatians chapter 5.
However, in the original Greek, the word "faith" in Galatians 5:22 could be translated faithfulness. The fruit of the Spirit are for character; the gifts of the Spirit are for power. Fruit is something that grows. Faith — or faithfulness — is a fruit that grows in the life of a Christian to establish him in godly spiritual character. But the gift of faith is a special gift which is given supernaturally by the Spirit of God, as He wills. Those who operate in special faith, the gift of the Spirit, can believe God in such a way that God honors their word as His own, and miraculously brings to pass the desired result. Thus, we learn that there are different kinds of faith. Saving faith brings one to salvation. Faith or faithfulness, the fruit of the Spirit, comes after salvation. And the manifestation of the gift of special faith can come as a gift of the Spirit after one receives the baptism in the Holy Ghost.

However, the gift of faith, which is a gift of the Spirit, operates as He wills, not as we will. Faith, like prayer, is something that is easily confused in the minds of some people. Many times, we just put all kinds of faith in the

same sack, so to speak, mix them up, and shake them all out together. But we must differentiate between saving faith, or the general faith that every believer has, and this special faith that God gives on certain occasions. Referring to general or saving faith, I have heard people say, "Well, if God gives me faith I will have it, and if He doesn't I won't." They read the scripture, "To another [is given] faith ..." (1
Cor. 12:9), and they think that is the way all faith works.

However, as we have already proven, this special faith, this gift of faith, is not the same saving faith or general faith which one needs in order to be saved. And special faith is not the faith needed for believing God to have your needs met according to His Word. The faith for believing God for your needs to be met comes by hearing the Word (Rom. 10:17), and every believer is given a measure of that kind of faith (Rom. 12:3).

Also, as I already pointed out, this gift of faith is not the fruit of faith that grows in a person's life to develop character in Christian living. Special faith is not the general faith by which we ordinarily receive answers to prayer. We know that we are saved by general faith; we know that we receive the baptism in the Holy Ghost by faith — general faith. We know that we receive answers to prayer by this kind of ordinary or general faith because Jesus said, ". . . What things soever ye desire, when ye pray, believe that ye receive them, and ye shall have them"(Mark 11:24).

Many of us have received many answers to prayer just through faith even before we ever received the baptism in the Holy Ghost. These answers came because we believed God and appropriated the promises in His Word by faith. But that is still not this gift of faith as described in First Corinthians 12:9.

If the gift of faith had to be in manifestation in order to get an answer to prayer, to receive the baptism of the Holy Ghost, to receive healing for your body, or to have a financial need met, then you could never get your prayers answered until after you got saved and received the baptism in the Holy Ghost. Yet many of us, including myself, did receive healing before we ever received the baptism of the Holy Ghost; we received healing by exercising simple faith in
what God's Word says.

Also, if these general answers to prayer were the result of the gift of faith in operation, then not everyone — even if they had the baptism in the Holy Ghost — would be able to obtain answers to prayer, because not everyone will have this gift operating in them. Remember, the Bible says, "For to ONE is given by the Spirit the word of wisdom. . .. To another faith by the same
Spirit" (1 Cor. 12:8,9).
Therefore, if we had to rely on this gift of faith to get our prayers answered, then not everyone could get

their prayers answered, and we know that is untrue. But there is a faith — I call it a general faith — that all believers have that can be increased by feeding on the Word of God and exercising it in the arena of life. We can all have an ever-increasing faith. The gift of faith, however, is a supernatural manifestation of the Holy Spirit given as the Spirit wills."
The Holy Spirit and His Gifts Kenneth E Hagin pgs. 151-152

Chapter Four
Judging the Holy Spirit Gift of Prophecy

Here is the New Testament definition for the gift of prophecy:
1 Corinthians 14:3
3 But he that prophesieth speaketh unto men to edification, and exhortation, and comfort.

The Word of God is not up to debate, so this not a statement on its cessation or continuation. It is a single sentence which defines the gift of prophecy as it existed in the first century Church. You can not deny it's existence back then, only the apostle Paul was teaching the Church about its function. Here are the facts 1) Prophecy is not preaching or teaching of the Scriptures. 2) Prophecy is not a special discernment given to rightly divide the written Word of God. 3) Prophecy is one of the gifts of the Holy Spirit which speaks to men in a know language. If you are English speaking a word of prophecy will given in the English language. The simple gift of prophecy has "no supernatural revelation," like a future prediction, or revelation of present-day facts. 4) The simple gift of prophecy only has three elements when spoken by inspiration of the Holy Spirit. 5) The 3 elements are edification, exhortation, and comfort. Only those elements spoken in a prophetic word is recognized as the simple gift of prophecy.

The apostle Paul also states the purpose of the Holy Spirit gift of prophecy.
1 Corinthians 14:4
4 He that speaketh in an unknown tongue edifieth himself; but he that prophesieth edifieth the church.

The original intent of the gift of prophecy was to edify the Church by a spoken word which came from the inspiration of the Holy Spirit. Prophecy in its simplest form was not preaching, or predicting the future, or visions of heaven, or angelic visitations it is a born-again Christians speaking a simple word of encouragement inspired by the Holy Spirit. This gift existed in the first century Church and the apostle Paul encouraged the whole Church to desire the gift of prophecy. Never did Paul put prophecy on equal authority as the Written Word of God, neither did Paul teach we were to despise Prophecy.

1 Corinthians 14:39-40
39 Wherefore, brethren, covet to prophesy, and forbid not to speak with tongues.
40 Let all things be done decently and in order.

Now does the gift of prophecy exist today in modern Charismatics? Let's start with a statement many are the thousands who are saying the have a prophetic word from God. Is it the simple gift of prophecy as stated by Paul in teaching the Church at Corinth? I would say 95 % of modern prophetic words are about the future, or dreams, or visions, or visitations which are not the simple gift of prophecy. All most gone from existence is "the Holy Spirit inspired simple gift of prophecy given as the Lord wills." Today the Charismatic Church is overrun by mystical experiences which is labeled as the Prophetic or the Extreme Prophetic. Also has pushed the Biblical definition of prophecy out from its Biblical restraints Into the New Age and occult. Simply put you will not garner large audiences or big money, and labels of being characterized as a prophet, by encouraging the Church with the simple gift of prophecy.

What is the problem? Most of those who are called modern day prophets are not truly prophesying by the Holy Spirit gift of prophecy as defined by the first century Church. Since the modern gift of New Testament of prophesy does not center in anyone man, no man can become the center of attention with all other Christians attempting g to "follow the prophet."

The true gift would be distributed throughout the whole body of Christ, so no man could claim a corner on prophetic words. Instead, the Holy Spirit would lead the inspiration choosing the member of the body of belivers who would be inspired to prophecy in anyone meeting to encourage, exhort, and strengthen the saints present. In the Charismatic Movement of the 1980's this is how the simple gift of prophecy functioned.

The change began when the boundaries which defined the gift of prophecy were violated by what is called the Extreme Prophetic. Today the Charismatic Church stands idly by and watches prophetic superstars who have the word of the Lord for them. Basically, fortune telling has subverted the leading of the Holy Spirit giving a platform for thousands of false prophetic words. So, am I supposed to submit to an inerrant false prophetic ministry which has fallen to New Age and occult practices? In no way should anyone subject themselves. Charismatics attempt to justify the prophetic ministry of today as Biblically accurate. In this case a Christian who challenges the gift of prophecy is not in existence today according to Bible standards is basically correct. However, the reason is not the gift of prophecy has passed away after the first century Church. Instead, the Charismatic Movement have so perverted it as to become a danger to the authentic Christian faith.

Today Charismatics have their flesh pumped up by words of prophecy which are vain glory and itch their ears according to their ungodly lusts and desires. Speaking In the Name of the Lord

Since the Charismatic Movement has been exposed with giving false prophecies, why couldn't those false prophecies have been judged before the name of the Lord was defiled? How could any Christian know for sure if a prophetic word has originated with the Holy Spirit? What standard of measure has been given to the Church to judge prophecies? First, no man is given a right to speak in the name of the Lord by his own private interpretations. No special revelation which come from new interpretations of Scriptures are allowed. This has been the major issue inside the Charismatic Movement which are private interpretations being put as "new light" of worn-out doctrinal beliefs. Especially in relationship to end time judgments and the Second Coming of the Lord. Instead of preaching or teaching doctrine about end times, the Prophetic Movement has practiced predicting prophetically end time events. If Charismatics could really see 99% of their predictions are philosophical beliefs being prophesied in the name of the Lord. Instead of preaching or teaching their position, Charismatics use the name of the Lord to bring credibility.

When judging prophecy, one can see if the prophecy is really a doctrinal statement as compared to a prophetic word. The Scriptures do not allow for new doctrines to spoken as prophecy. As New Testament prophecy is a gift of the Holy Spirit, and not to develop new doctrines. The Holy Spirit would never speak against what has already been written in the Word of God. The Charismatic Prophetic Movement is constantly violating this principle, by bringing in private interpretation, and new revelations which cannot be supported by what is written in the Scriptures.

Here is a safety measure when testing a prophetic word. Does it violate Gods written word and will? A prophetic word should not undermine the Scriptures in any way. In judging a prophetic word, Christians should be able to point to the doctrines in the Scriptures as support and measurement. For example, prophecy would never falsely lift up a man exposing him to being glorified and idolized. Yet, many charismatic words have been guilty of exalting a man into a position God has never intended and is rebuked by Scriptures. Man-made wisdom and glorification are often put off as a prophetic word and can be easily discerned as coming from a man's flesh, and not the Holy Spirit gift of prophecy.

The gift of prophecy as written in Scriptures is a word spoken by inspiration of the Holy Spirit, for edification, exhortation, and comfort. When the Prophetic

Movement attempted to go beyond the Biblical gift of prophecy, a false practice was introduced and normalized. Instead of the gift of prophecy, supernatural experiences were substituted. These manifestations were labeled as the "extreme prophetic," and introduced New Age spirituality into the Charismatic Prophetic Movement. In fact, the major leaders of the Prophetic Movement have taught the New Age was stolen from the Church and must be recovered. Now days the false prophetic includes Charismatics using tarot cards and predicting the future. Instead of the gift of prophecy psychic manifestations coming from soul power are now called words of prophecy.

New Age is a form of witchcraft using soul powers, as the result evil spirits have invaded the Prophetic Movement. Today, a Charismatic might be taught New Age practices like spirit travel, where a man can leave his body and travel by his spirit. Others might teach how to travel by mystical portals into heaven. Communication with the dead, and angels, and visions upon demand all have tapped into psychic and New Age powers. All these manifestations are labeled as prophetic ministry, and all manner of lying dreams, visions, and angels of light have invaded the Movement. Without restraint from the true gift of prophecy, and the Written Word of God, the Prophetic Movement has become a haven of deception and error as demonstrated by the hundreds of false and lying predictions which have exposed their prophets.

1. Until the standard of Scriptures is restored the true gift of prophecy will be lost to demonic counterfeits being passed off as the Word of the Lord.

Suppose you have common knowledge about situations, in which a great deal of people already knows about. Then you have a dream about that situation, or feel God wants you to speak about those know facts. I have a choice, I can just talk about it without trying to "make it a prophet word," instead just speaking about my concerns in a typical teaching, preaching, or common communication way. If I wanted people to identify me "as a prophet," and I was always needing to "give a prophetic word," I can take what is known by common knowledge and put a "thus says the Lord," upon what I am saying. By doing this it leads the Church to believe the word I am speaking has come by revelation knowledge. What am I really doing, I want to be known as a prophet, and I am subtly "marketing my gifting," so I can gain acceptance as a prophet whom God speaks through, and gain an audience? Of course, this is selfish ambition, and misuse of the prophetic gifting by self-promotion.

Now what if I did not "attach a God has shown me label," to the very same correction? Instead, I just warn the leaders about the cost of immorality, idolatry of ministry, and exploitation of the Church for personal profit? I do not have the same wight of authority, in the eyes of the people. Even though its correct to confront sin, leaders can they just say, it is your own personal opinion, and I do not agree. Now, it is no longer a prophetic word, or the weight of a prophet, instead it is a Christian leader bringing correction. Simply put you do not need to be a prophet in the Church to confront and correct sin. Also, you can be sure, God is judging immorality, pride, greed, and idolatry of ministry in all the Church.

What is the problem with the prophetic ministry today? The pressure to preform and give prophetic words to demonstrate you are a prophet. So many words which are given as a word of the Lord, have behind them ministry ambition and promotion. Just look at all the prophets who want to sell the revelations, in platform, or marketing, or bestselling books. I would say any Christian who is always identifying as a prophet is off center to begin with. As their identity is in Christ, not in their ministry. I have seen this corruption for years in the prophetic and have participated in the sin and flesh through my own ministry. It is time for the prophets to see the marketing of revelation, the mysteries and secrets of God has drawn you away and into exploiting the Church "in the name of God."

1 Corinthians 14:29-40.
29 Let the prophets speak two or three and let the other judge.
30 If any thing be revealed to another that sitteth by, let the first hold his peace.
31 For ye may all prophesy one by one, that all may learn, and all may be comforted.
32 And the spirits of the prophets are subject to the prophets.
33 For God is not the author of confusion, but of peace, as in all churches of the saints.
34 Let your women keep silence in the churches: for it is not permitted unto them to speak; but they are commanded to be under obedience, as also saith the law.
35 And if they will learn any thing, let them ask their husbands at home: for it is a shame for women to speak in the church.
36 What? came the word of God out from you? or came it unto you only?
37 If any man think himself to be a prophet, or spiritual, let him acknowledge that the things that I write unto you are the commandments of the Lord.
38 But if any man be ignorant, let him be ignorant.
39 Wherefore, brethren, covet to prophesy, and forbid not to speak with tongues.
40 Let all things be done decently and in order.

5 Easy Steps to Judge a Prophetic Word

In today's world of prophetic ministry many false prophecies abound, so the Scriptures teach New Testament Prophecy must be tested and judged as to its authenticity. First, all prophetic words must originate from God Himself, and not by the will of man. Here in lies a great difficulty as many Charismatic Christians attempt to give a prophetic word which originates from their own will and desire. Even more perilous are prophetic words spoken by psychic ability which can have an element of truth, but its origin comes from psychic powers and not from the Holy Spirit. As the result prophetic words must be tested and tested for the Spirit by which it has been given. If a prophetic word is proven to not come from the Holy Spirit, no matter how accurate the details it must be rejected completely as many difficulties can arise by following false prophecies.

1 Corinthians 14:29-33
29 Let the prophets speak two or three and let the other judge.
30 If any thing be revealed to another that sitteth by, let the first hold his peace.
31 For ye may all prophesy one by one, that all may learn, and all may be comforted.
32 And the spirits of the prophets are subject to the prophets.

33 For God is not the author of confusion, but of peace, as in all churches of the saints.

Step 1: Does It violate the Scriptures

Step 2: Does it Glorify Man or God

Step 3: Does It Witness to the Person Receiving the Prophecy

Step 4: Does It Bring Edification, Exhortation and Comfort

Step 5: Does It Witness to the Holy Spirit

Revelation Knowledge, False Predictions, Psychic Ability

Authentic revelation knowledge given by the Holy Spirit does not add or subtract from what has already been written in Scriptures. So, if I say I had a vision Jesus Christ said for me to rewrite the Bible adding or subtracting words from the Scriptures, then a demonic spirit is impersonating Jesus Christ. The gifts of the Holy Spirit are subordinate to the doctrines of the Bible, and no additional "new revelation" is given as a hidden mystery never before seen or understood. Why is so much effort put forth for modern "prophets to predict the future." In this way they can say I have access to God in a way others do not have. What is the problem with this practice? A man who is constantly predicting the future is not manifesting the Holy Spirits gifts of revelation. Neither are they a New Testament Prophet with the gift of sight called a seer. Notice any Old Testament prophet who brought a futuristic word of prophecy spoke of Gods judgment upon Israel. The Old Testament Seer was a prophet of judgement who foresaw Gods future judgments. I am convinced those who proclaim they are the New Testament version of Seers are the same who have preached a false Gospel.

The Holy Spirit has not given them the Word of Wisdom which reveals future events. As the Holy Spirit manifests the gift of the word of wisdom by His administration, according to Gods discretion and will. No man can say upon demand I will now function in seeing the future upon my will and demand. Any man who is constantly building their ministries upon future predictions has drawn an audience who do not know the leading of the Holy Spirit for themselves. You do not function like a New Testament prophet or seer who is leading men and women to a deeper relationship with Jesus Christ. Instead, you function more like a psychic, with powers of fortune telling, the psychic ability to predict the future. The revelatory power you have tapped is power of the soul. As you have violated the boundaries which govern and protect the gifts of the Holy Spirit constantly opening your soul to forces which are under your control, and do not come from God.

Ignorant Charismatics who cannot discern psychic powers from the gifts of the Holy Spirit are into your folly. As your meetings are about predictions, and manifestations of supernatural facts. The doctrines of Jesus Christ have little relevance in your meetings and your audience has not come to hear you preach the Gospel, or the doctrines of Christ. Instead, you choose to manifest secrets, and secret knowledge which are declared to be words of knowledge or wisdom by the Holy Spirit. You can acquire their names, birth dates, home addresses which prove you are "hearing from God." Except God is not in fortune telling, or psychic soul power, or familiar spirits, or astral travel, or anything else you can do upon your own will and demand.

God already knows everything about you and does not need to prove to you He has omniscience by revealing your name, address, or birthdate. Instead, God is interested in your growth and maturation into Sonship through solid foundations and walk of faith by the leading of the Holy Spirit. God is not going to tickle your flesh with sensuous manifestations. The gifts of the Holy Spirit will only strengthen your walk in the Lord, and not pump up your flesh.

Words of wisdom can show the future like what was given the prophet Daniel. God can give the knowledge of facts which are clearly shown supernaturally as true facts. The word of Knowledge can reveal modern day facts or history in a supernatural way. These manifestations are only given by the Holy Spirit and are not under the control of man. A man who is constantly giving visions has opened his soul to counterfeits and has a history of failed predictions. In the Charismatic Movement you can name them by name, just check their most previous prophetic predictions. You will see all the backpedaling they are now doing to justify why they gave another false prophecy. Yet they want everyone to declare they are a prophet of the Lord.

Despise Not Prophesying

The apostle Paul in reproving the error of beliefs about the Second Coming finished by saying, do not quench the Holy Spirit, and do not despise prophesying. Prove all things, hold fast that which is good. Abstain all appearance of evil. The modern Church of Charismatics have then used this passage to allow false prophesy as a normal course of sifting out prophetic words. The thought being by rejecting prophecy you will quench the Holy Spirit. Is this the true meaning of what quenching the Holy Spirit to accept a great deal of false prophetic predictions for in the process a true word of the Lord may be present?

I have a question, why wouldn't Christians despise false Prophecy? Doesn't the admonition to test the spirits, to prove all things then suggest Christians can know the true from the false?

Why would the Scriptures warn of the false prophets who work by a spirit of error, and Christians have an anointing to overcome them? How dangerous are the false prophecies which come from men inside the Church? In not despising prophecy was Paul saying not to despise false prophesy. In no way can Christians be in any agreement with false prophets and false prophesy. Do you love a lie, even if it were to come in a form which says God showed me, or God told me? Where in Scriptures are we told to compromise with the Spirit of truth and accept false prophesy to have the true too.

This I am sure of false prophecy of any kind is not to be tolerated in fear of quenching the Spirit. As false prophesy did not originate with the Holy Spirit and has behind them deep ramifications which also include evil spirits at work in the Church. Any man who gives a failed predictive word should take a serious look into their motives, and reasons to minister the word of the Lord. I am very sure Paul was not asking Christians to accept false prophecy along side the true the way it is practiced in the modern charismatic church of today.

Instead, Paul was asking Christians not to despise authentic prophecy. Real prophecy from the Lord in Paul's day would have asked Christians to endure the hardships, trails, and tests which caused great suffering in their day. So severe was the persecution of the first century Church many had thought they were in the Great Tribulation, and Caesar Nero was the Antichrist.

Prophetic words were likely to encourage and exhort the saints to endure until the end. Many would suffer the loss of all things in keeping their testimony in the face of persecution and threat of martyrdom. Prophecy from the Holy Spirit was not a false prediction of politics like we hear today. So many failed Charismatics prophetic predictions come from a philosophical belief. Building a whole theology based upon government and politics.

If you miss a predictive word of prophecy, especially after trying to convince the Church you are a prophet of God its serious business. You have quenched the Holy Spirit by misleading the body of Christ who have foolishly put their trust in your reputation as a prophet. The Scriptures warns how false prophets will deceive the people leading many astray by great swelling words of vanity. Any time a man who claims to be a prophet of God gives a false prediction, the Church should warn of serious deception and error. After all the Holy Spirit is the Spirit of Truth and would never lead anyone to speak falsely in the name of the Lord. Any supposed prophet who refused to admit deception and refuses to repent has surely grieved the Holy Spirit and will be judged by God.

1 Thessalonians 5:19-23
19 Quench not the Spirit.
20 Despise not prophesyings.
21 Prove all things; hold fast that which is good.

22 Abstain from all appearance of evil.
23 And the very God of peace sanctify you wholly; and I
pray God your whole spirit and soul and body be
preserved blameless unto the coming of
our Lord Jesus Christ.

Part II Who Is the Holy Spirit

Chapter Five.
The Holy Spirit as God

Sometimes Christians don't really understand the
significance of the Holy Spirit being God. Perhaps this is
why the Charismatic Movement suffers so much from
the false prophetic. As many so-called prophets like to
speak of their angelic visitations to draw a big audience.
What is ironic about Charismatics following the words
which come from angels is the number of lying
visitations and false words supposedly spoken by angels
in the name of the Lord. Why would God begin to
emphasize angels when the born-again Christian are
filled with the Holy Spirit of God? How inferior are
angels to God, why minimize the Holy Spirit to promote
angels. The truth be told, its pure deception to follow
the Charismatic Prophets and their supposed angelic
visitations. Let's be frank, angels do the bidding for the
Lord, and the Holy Spirit is the Lord God.

What did Jesus Christ mean when He said of the Holy Spirit He would come as "another Comforter?" To this point Jesus had been leading His disciples and had been their source of encouragement and comfort. "Another Comforter," in this case would be God in the Spirit. Where Jesus Christ is God in the flesh, the Holy Spirit of God would come to abide with the disciples "forever." In this case "another is "coequal, coeternal, and consubstantial" as God, equal to God the Son, and God the Father.

John 14:16

[16] And I will pray the Father, and he shall give you another Comforter, that he may abide with you forever; Another huge mistake is to make the Holy Spirit an atmosphere, a presence, a feeling, a force. God is a Spirit, and actual person with divine character and nature. The failure to not recognize the Holy Spirit as the "person of God," has led to a great deal of charismatic deception. The reality of heaven coming to earth has "already happened" when do you ask? Say not in your heart who shall ascend into heaven that is to bring Christ down? As God has already come to earth to save with the Cross of Jesus Christ. Then again heaven came to earth to remain on the Day of Pentecost to remain as God the Holy Spirit came to indwell believers.

Now understand the difference with the Holy Spirit indwelling born again Christians, and the false doctrine of "heaven to earth." Do you not know your body is the Temple of the Holy Spirit, and the Spirit of God indwells you? How close is God when by His Holy Spirit He indwells the bodies of His saints? Is not the "center of Heaven all about God Himself?"

Let's get real, Gods Spirit has made the body of born Christians a temple, the place where He can dwell. Now God dwells in Heaven on His throne, and will never bring heaven to earth, instead has given God the Holy Spirt to dwell with the saints forever. It will never be the false doctrine of the Church bringing heaven to earth as taught by the apostles of the NAR Charismatic Movement. The atmosphere or environment Gods wants to transform by His Holy Spirit is the one inside your body, transforming you into the likeness of Jesus Christ. When you are being transformed on the inside from glory to glory into the image of Jesus Christ this is the true effect of God by His Spirit into your life.

The other, is the false Gospel of bringing heaven to earth which undermines the Cross and denies the true work of the Holy Spirit. The false Gospel wants to transform the "atmosphere" with a God feeling instead gives place to the Prince of the Power of the Air to imitate the presence of God. That false Gospel is full of deception and unbelief playacting like its super spirituality.

John 14:16-31

16 And I will pray the Father, and he shall give you another Comforter, that he may abide with you forever;

17 Even the Spirit of truth; whom the world cannot receive, because it seeth him not, neither knoweth him: but ye know him; for he dwelleth with you, and shall be in you.

18 I will not leave you comfortless: I will come to you.

19 Yet a little while, and the world seeth me no more; but ye see me: because I live, ye shall live also.

20 At that day ye shall know that I am in my Father, and ye in me, and I in you.

21 He that hath my commandments, and keepeth them, he it is that loveth me: and he that loveth me shall be loved of my Father, and I will love him, and will manifest myself to him.   22 Judas saith unto him, not Iscariot, Lord, how is it that thou wilt manifest thyself unto us, and not unto the world?

23 Jesus answered and said unto him, If a man love me, he will keep my words: and my Father will love him, and we will come unto him, and make our abode with him.

24 He that loveth me not keepeth not my sayings: and the word which ye hear is not mine, but the Father's which sent me.

25 These things have I spoken unto you, being yet present with you.

26 But the Comforter, which is the Holy Ghost, whom the Father will send in my name, he shall teach you all

things, and bring all things to your remembrance, whatsoever I have said unto you.

²⁷ Peace I leave with you, my peace I give unto you: not as the world giveth, give I unto you. Let not your heart be troubled, neither let it be afraid.

²⁸ Ye have heard how I said unto you, I go away, and come again unto you. If ye loved me, ye would rejoice, because I said, I go unto the Father: for my Father is greater than I.

²⁹ And now I have told you before it come to pass, that, when it is come to pass, ye might believe.

³⁰ Hereafter I will not talk much with you: for the prince of this world cometh, and hath nothing in me.

³¹ But that the world may know that I love the Father; and as the Father gave me commandment, even so I do. Arise, let us go hence.

ChapterSix
The Holy Spirit as Spirit of Truth

When we speak of the Holy Spirit, we are speaking of the 3rd person of the Godhead, God the Spirit. The Holy Spirit is no less God, than God the Father, or God the Son. Therefore, the Holy Spirit being God in totality, in character, in person, makes it impossible for the Holy Spirit to lie. Another impossibility for the Holy Spirit, is it's impossible for the Spirit not to know. As God is omniscient, God knows all things without limit all the time. Therefore, the Holy Spirit can never lead a Christian into deception, or into corruption, or into lies.

However, many Charismatics seem to think Gods knowledge is limited especially when they speak falsely in the name of the Lord giving a false prophetic prediction. False prophetic words are backed up by excuse's which seem to say God did not know wither or not the prophetic word would actually come to past.

The excuse goes something like the Church failed to pray to bring that prophetic word to pass. God already knew the complete outcome of any event on earth from the beginning to the end. As God Himself dwells outside of time and has always been and ever will be eternal. The problem with false prophetic words lies entirely with the man or woman who "misspoke in the name of the Lord." It become a sad state of affairs when the secular media must correct the integrity of the Charismatic Movement exposing all the false predictions given in the name of the Lord. What a reproach in the name of the Lord when Christians give fake prophetic words, and then blame the Church or attack the omniscience of the Holy Spirit.

How is it when God spoke through the prophets of old, their prophetic predictions withstood the test of time, culture, morality, and advancements in technology. Today, prophetic words are mostly subjective based upon predicting the outcomes of circumstances. They ring hollow, have very little "eternal weight," are mostly sensational based upon impressing a Charismatic audience. Let's compare the apostle John who was banished to the Island of Patmos where the Holy Spirit gave John the visions of the apocalypse and the end of this age. The Church at that time was going through terrible persecution at the hands of the Roman Cesar's. Do you think any Christians were looking for a golden age of the Church, and a worldwide Church takeover? The truth was the Church for the first two hundred years was completely pre-Millennial. As the result of deep suffering Christians often thought the Great Tribulation was at hand. However, John was given the visions of the Apocalypse which are now about 1800 years removed from their inception.

Did God the Holy Spirit make a mistake, and not understand how long the Church would exist to "make for a Christian world?" For today you see Charismatics who are called apostles and prophets speak of a great worldwide Church Christianization of nations. Did the Holy Spirit not know the truth of world history, and technological advancements which would improve the world, making for a better man, and a better world? Is the Apocalypse given to John almost 2000 years ago now not relevant for today's modern Church and world? How deep the divide from modern day apostolic Charismatics who say they "have new light" on old worn-out interpretations of the book of Revelation. Which means the original Church in the days of apostle John were more easily deceived and not as astute in spiritual matters as modern-day Charismatics. Of course, this just a big hog wash of lies, and a lying spirit allowed into todays Charismatic Movement.

The Testimony of Jesus is the Spirit of prophecy. God the Holy Spirit was completely knowledgeable of how long the Church would exist on earth, and the conditions which would exist at the end of this age. No lack of knowledge or understanding was absent from the visions John was given by the Holy Spirit in exact detail of the Second Coming of Jesus Christ. No matter if man has so advanced himself in technology and speaks of saving the world, or making for better weather, or extending the life spans. No number of circumstances will stop the more sure word of prophecies given in the book of Revelation which speaks of 21 end time catastrophic judgments.

I for one have grown weary of all the big and little lies spoken in the name of God, which are being passed off as the work of the Holy Spirit. I'll just stay with what the apostle John was given from "the Eternal Spirit of God," and not join in darkening the character and nature of God every time another false prophetic prediction is exposed by Newsweek Magazine, and the Washington Post. Since the apostles and prophets have grown to accept lies and lying in the name of the Lord, I figure they don't know much about the true person of the Holy Spirit, the Spirit of Truth. If they are ignorant of the character and nature of the Holy Spirit, why so assured to "speak in the name of the Lord?" As it's not Gods testimony, then just who is really speaking all those lies?

John 15:16-27
16 Ye have not chosen me, but I have chosen you, and ordained you, that ye should go and bring forth fruit, and that your fruit should remain: that whatsoever ye shall ask of the Father in my name, he may give it you.
17 These things I command you, that ye love one another.
18 If the world hate you, ye know that it hated me before it hated you.
19 If ye were of the world, the world would love his own: but because ye are not of the world, but I have chosen you out of the world, therefore the world hateth you.
20 Remember the word that I said unto you, The servant is not greater than his lord. If they have persecuted me, they will also persecute you; if they have kept my saying, they will keep yours also.
21 But all these things will they do unto you for my name's sake, because they know not him that sent me.
22 If I had not come and spoken unto them, they had not had sin: but now they have no cloke for their sin.
23 He that hateth me hateth my Father also.
24 If I had not done among them the works which none other man did, they had not had sin: but now have they both seen and hated both me and my Father.

25 But this cometh to pass, that the word might be fulfilled that is written in their law, They hated me without a cause.
26 But when the Comforter is come, whom I will send unto you from the Father, even the Spirit of truth, which proceedeth from the Father, he shall testify of me:
27 And ye also shall bear witness, because ye have been with me from the beginning.

The Holy Spirit and Written Word of God

Today seems like if you are a Charismatic a great divide has come with those who are pursuing experiences of the supernatural kind, and Charismatics who hold strictly to the written Word of God. The Bible clearly teaches experiences which are foundational when it comes to the works of the Holy Spirit. If you are born again of the Holy Spirit, you will see the New Testament Scriptures completely confirms this work of the Holy Spirit as an "orthodox supernatural experience." No person can rightly attack the "born again work of Salvation," as without the born again experience no man is become a child of God. You must be born again of the Holy Spirit to appropriate the Blood of the Cross for your justification and forgiveness before God. Also, the born-again experience gives the "new creation," renewing the human spirit making for a new creation man made anew in Christ.

What if you speak in tongues is this part of the born-again experience? Technically speaking, a man, or woman can receive a new creation born again experience without speaking in tongues. As Salvation is not related to speaking in tongues so a Christian can be saved without receiving the gift of speaking in tongues. Is speaking in tongues then not orthodox? Absolutely not, the Gifts of the Holy Spirit are clearly written in the Scriptures as an orthodox Holy Spirit experience. No man has the right to declare the Gifts of the Holy Spirit as extra Biblical supernatural manifestations, as the Bible teaches Christians to desire the Gifts of the Holy Spirit including speaking in tongues.

The only true reliable guide to "tests the spirits" to see if these supernatural experiences are truly Biblical, as is the Written Word of God. Now days modern Charismatics want to "attack" the limits and boundaries of supernatural as written in the Scriptures. The problem today with Charismatics is to treat everything which is declared as a supernatural experience having its origin from God. However, many things which are happening in the Charismatic Movement today cannot be found in the Written Word of God. What does it mean? The supernatural has invaded the Charismatic Church leading Christians into experiences which have no redemptive value, as those supernatural encounters "just dead end" in themselves with no real fruit which brings increase in the Spirit.

For example, if a man is born again after hearing the Gospel of Salvation this is completely Biblical found as doctrine in the Written Word of God. If a man hears of the Gift of the Holy Spirit, and wants to be filled with the Holy Spirit, and begins to speak in tongues is this orthodox also? This too is easily tested by the Written Word of God as it is also written as doctrine in the Bible. However, if I say I am an apostle who had a visitation from Jesus taken into the library of heaven, this is to be "tested as an extra biblical experience," and should not just be blindly accepted by Charismatics as coming from God.

Now if in the visitation the supposed apostle says, Jesus commissioned me to rewrite the Bible, and the Bible is not yet complete as John chapter 22 is still in heaven, only to be revealed to the Church to make the world Christian. How are Christians to judge or test this as a work of God? First of all, it is completely against the Written Word of God as no new light of revelation is to be added or subtracted from the Written Word of God. Any supposed "apostle" who adds words to the Bible or takes them away has come under Gods curse. How am I to judge the experience of this man going into heaven? As a Satanic lying supernatural experience, as Satan can produce supernatural experiences too, and often mimics these experiences as if it is the Holy Spirit, or Jesus, or an angel sent from God.

Is the man who is called an apostle, who has a vision which violates which has already been written in the Word of God being "accused," or attacked when confronted by Christians as a false apostle? The man is clearly deceived fallen to the snare of Satan even if he is truly born again. In the Christian faith all supernatural experiences are tested by the Written Word of God. If a man no matter an apostle, or a prophet, or teacher, or Church leader won't repent of violating the Written Word of God, this man or woman must be marked by the Church and avoided. As the Holy Spirit will never violate what has been written in the Word of God, as the Word of God and the Holy Spirit are in complete agreement. For the final authority of authentic Holy Spirit supernatural experiences rests within the Scriptures, and not with experiences alone.

2 Timothy 3:13-17

[13] But evil men and seducers shall wax worse and worse, deceiving, and being deceived.

[14] But continue thou in the things which thou hast learned and hast been assured of, knowing of whom thou hast learned
them;

[15] And that from a child thou hast known the holy scriptures, which are able to make thee wise unto salvation through faith which is in Christ
Jesus.

[16] All scripture is given by inspiration of God, and is

profitable for doctrine, for reproof, for correction, for instruction in righteousness:

[17] That the man of God may be perfect, thoroughly furnished unto all good works.

Chapter Seven
The Holy Spirit Our Teacher

The Scriptures teach the Holy Spirit is not only our Guide, and the Holy Spirit is also our teacher. The Holy Spirit is the Spirit of Truth who leads and guides us into all truth. Why is this important? The prevailing influences of false teachers, and false doctrines has made it a necessary part of the Church Universal to have the Holy Spirit expose all the deception. When false teachers abound and go unchallenged the Holy Spirit is being suppressed in the Church. No matter how spiritual or how popular the teacher of false doctrines, that Church has grieved the Holy Spirit. For false teachers function in the antichrist spirit, and the spirit of error speaking against the Holy Spirit of Truth.

In the last times, and as the last days approach many false prophets are arising within the Church. They went out from the Church as many are the Christians who have fallen to the snare of the Devil and are leading the Church astray by man made philosophies. But you have an unction, for the Holy Spirit, the "Chrisma" by the Spirit who teaches you all things. This unction given by the Holy Spirit will testify of the Lord and bring to your remembrance the things which Jesus Christ has spoken.

When false teachers are manifesting a false teaching the unction of the Holy Spirit inside you will "teach you," give witnesses what is being taught in not from God. As much as the modern Charismatic Church likes to point out supernatural manifestations related to the "charisma" of the Holy Spirit, they all but deny the Charisma of the Holy Spirit which exposes the deception of guiding into all Truth.

What is ironic, are how false apostles and false prophets want to act today as if they are so filled with the Holy Spirit. They put on a show as if the have received "new light of revelation" which they say God has showed, or God has spoken. However, what they say is against the Testimony of Jesus the Spirit of Prophecy, and they speak by spirit of error. Their deluded mind has given place to demonic seduction as they are tempted to believe they have been given "something special from God." Which makes them elite, seeing something no other Christian-has seen before. However, the Holy Spirit on the inside of born-again Christians will expose the pride and deception from which this man's temptation has produced this doctrine of demons. The Holy Spirit will expose the deception, and the pride as the reason this false teacher has given place to evil spirits. Of course, it's taking the anointing of the Holy

Spirit to teach these things, and to show us the deception.

Is the Holy Spirit grieved in modern day Charismatic Movements who refuse correction from false doctrines and even heresies? Are these men attacking those who confront them by discerning the false doctrines by having the Holy Spirit teach them the Truth. These things are written as our admonition and instruction, that no lie is of the truth. No matter how popular apostles and prophets attempt to seduce the Church by their charisma and charm.

1 John 2:18-29
18 Little children, it is the last time: and as ye have heard that antichrist shall come, even now are there many antichrists; whereby we know that it is the last time.
19 They went out from us, but they were not of us; for if they had been of us, they would no doubt have continued with us: but they went out, that they might be made manifest that they were not all of us.
20 But ye have an unction from the Holy One, and ye know all things.
21 I have not written unto you because ye know not the truth, but because ye know it, and that no lie is of the truth.
22 Who is a liar but he that denieth that Jesus is the Christ? He is antichrist, that denieth the Father and the Son.

23 Whosoever denieth the Son, the same hath not the Father: .
24 Let that therefore abide in you, which ye have heard from the beginning. If that which ye have heard from the beginning shall remain in you, ye also shall continue in the Son, and in the Father.
25 And this is the promise that he hath promised us, even eternal life.
26 These things have I written unto you concerning them that seduce you.
27 But the anointing which ye have received of him abideth in you, and ye need not that any man teach you: but as the same anointing teacheth you of all things, and is truth, and is no lie, and even as it hath taught you, ye shall abide in him.
28 And now, little children, abide in him; that, when he shall appear, we may have confidence, and not be ashamed before him at his coming.
29 If ye know that he is righteous, ye know that everyone that doeth righteousness is born of him.

ChapterEight
Being Led of the Spirit

In all prophetic ministry Christians should be led of the Holy Spirit and not work after the efforts of the flesh. Learning how to be led of the Holy Spirit is a big part of growing up in the prophetic ministry.

Learning to divide the mind from the human spirit is helpful in being led of the Holy Spirit. As the indwelling of the Holy Spirit is in the new creation man, a born-again human spirit. While the mind is not born again it must be renewed by an increased understanding of God and the knowledge of His will. Studying the written Word of God can really help in learning to be led of the Spirit. As a Christian learns to hold his thoughts captive in his mind, casting down every lofty thought which exalts itself against the knowledge of God and obedience to Jesus Christ. So, walking after the Holy Spirit has a great deal about knowing the mind of Christ and guarding your heart and mind against thoughts and feelings which would lead you into temptation and away from the will of God. You must bring into the Cross your own, mind, will, and emotion crucifying your own lusts and affections submitting your will to the will of God.

Another important part of walking in the Spirit is to seek the Lord on daily basis. For those who fellowship with the Lord will be strengthened with the Holy Spirit in the inner man, the human spirit. Waiting upon the Lord in prayer will renew your strength and helps bring the flesh under the will of God. A daily prayer life helps us walk in the light as He is in the light having fellowship with the Lord as the blood of Jesus Christ cleanses us from all our sin. Waiting upon the Lord allows for the Holy Spirit to lead and guide us into all truth. The Holy Spirit will convict us of all unrighteousness so we can get our lives right. For as we confess our sins, He is faith and just to forgive us of our sins and to cleanse us from all unrighteousness. In walking in the Spirit sin brings an issue between us and the Lord, so it is important to apply the blood of Jesus Christ in confession of our sins to restore right relationship with Jesus Christ.

Keeping our relationship right with the Lord is extremely important to walking in the Spirit. Also, keeping our relationships with others is also important. The need to walk in love is instrumental to walking in the Spirit. Any evidence of hardness of heart, anger, unforgiveness are ways to grieve the Holy Spirit. We are to walk after the character and nature of the Lord, who demonstrated on the Cross ultimate forgiveness. How is it we have been forgiven so much at such a high price, the hold on to the offenses of our brothers in Christ. Even more we are to love our enemies, to bless and not curse, and pray for those who despitefully use and hurt our lives unjustly.

Ephesians 4:17-32
17 This I say therefore, and testify in the Lord, that
ye henceforth walk not as other Gentiles walk, in the of their mind,
18 Having the understanding darkened, being alienated from the life of God through the ignorance that
is in them, because of the blindness of their heart:
19 Who being past feeling have
given themselves over unto
lasciviousness, to work all uncleanness with greediness.

20 But ye have not so learned Christ;
21 If so be that ye have heard him, and have been
taught by him, as the truth is in Jesus:
22 That ye put off concerning the
former conversation the old man, which
is corrupt according to the deceitful lusts;
23 And be renewed in the spirit of your mind;
24 And that ye put on the new man, which after God is
created in righteousness and true holiness.
25 Wherefore putting away lying, speak every
man truth with his neighbour: for we are members one
of another.
26 Be ye angry, and sin not: let not the sun go
down upon your wrath:
27 Neither give place to the devil.
28 Let him that stole steal no more: but rather let
him labor, working with his hands the thing which
is good, that he may have to give to him that needeth.
29 Let no corrupt communication proceed out
of your mouth, but that which is good to the use of
edifying, that it may minister grace unto the hearers.
30 And grieve not the holy Spirit of God, whereby ye are
sealed unto the day of redemption.
31 Let all bitterness, and wrath, and anger, and clamour,
 and evil speaking, be put
away from you, with all malice:
32 And be
ye kind one to another, tenderhearted, forgiving one
another, even as God for Christ's sake hath
forgiven you.

Guidance From the Holy Spirit

First, I want to warn against being led by prophets' words. As everyone born of the Holy Spirit has the indwelling of the Spirit to led them. Letting prophetic words or prophets lead you is to revert to the Old Testament pattern where Israel did not have the born-again nature. So, God sent them prophets to help lead and guide them. Unfortunately, in the modern Charismatic Movement many have fallen into the practice of being led by Prophecy. Which has led many Charismatics out of the will of God for their lives.

Here are three factors to consider when seeking guidance from the Holy Spirit:

1) Does it agree with the written Word of God? As the Holy Spirit will never violate what has already been written in the Scriptures, anything which directs you to violate the Word of God is not guidance from God. Watch out for prophetic words which attempt to influence you in future decisions. For example, when prophet words attempt to say, "marry this person," or do this business. As the leading of the Lord should already be present in personal matters which are life changing matters like marriage and one's career.

2) The inner witness. As God has given us His Holy Spirit to lead us, Christians have the direction of

the Lord on the inside by their intuition. Watch out for following voices, as evil spirits will seduce you into following their imitation of Gods voice. Guidance from the Lord sometimes comes from the still small voice of the Lord, however most of the time it is just an inner witness without voices. Like green light to go, and red light to stop. Being lead of the Spirit in daily matters is more like this without any big seeking out what to eat, what to wear, just decide and do what you know what to do before God.

3) Gods Timing. Often Gods will be the same as your will and desires (when living right), however the timing and circumstances just do not line up. Being in the right time, and the right circumstances are often seen when God is opening the way. Even if it looks impossible to the natural circumstances when God is guiding, and it is His will and time these obstacles will not stop you. However, you might get out of Gods timing and attempt to do Gods will for your life out of time, out of season, and out of circumstances. It will only lead to your failure even though you were convinced God was guiding you by His Spirit. Many a failed Christian has launched out ahead of God and lost everything. It best to wait upon the Lord in major life decisions as God is never in a hurry.

Praying In the Holy Ghost
When seeking to be led of the Holy Spirit to seek
guidance on life decisions praying after the Holy Spirit is
important. Let take an example from the life of the
prophet Elijah. The prophetic ministry of Elijah is
featured both in the Old and New Testaments. The
relationship which the Prophet Elijah has with God is
featured in Elijah's ability to pray in the Spirit. Here is
the New Testament Scripture which teaches Christians
to pray after the manner of Elijah.

James 5:17-18
17 Elias was a man subject to like passions as we
are, and he prayed earnestly that it
might not rain: and it rained not on the earth by the
space of three years and six months.
18 And he prayed again, and the
heaven gave rain, and the earth brought forth her fruit.

Elijah was just a man subjected with all the human
weakness and limitations just like every other person.
The Scriptures teach the strength and ability in Elijah's
life was his ability to wait upon the Lord. After which
Elijah was able to pray in the Spirit according to the will
of God which caused great conviction and Israel turning
back to God. Why would God so honor the prayers of
Elijah? The answer comes from scriptures:

Elijah honored Gods Covenant with Israel and stood for
Lord calling His people out of idol worship and back into

relationship with the God of Israel. Elijah stood for the promises given to Abraham, Isaac, and Jacob. Elijah walked in the heart of God for Gods people seeking to restore Israel back to God as one who would pray for Gods mercy. However, Elijah would have to pronounce judgment which came from standing in the presence of God. In this way Elijah carried the burden of Israel and Elijah's prayers reflect his willingness to sacrifice his convenience in order to turn back Israel to God.

When confronting the prophets of Baal Elijah did exactly what God wanted with the evening sacrifice. How did Elijah know what to do? Elijah stood in the presence of the Lord to receive His council. This is also how Elijah's prayers moved heaven, as God already gave them Himself what to do and what to pray.

1 Kings 18:36-39
 And it came to pass at the time of the offering of the evening sacrifice, that Elijah prophet came, and said, Lord God of Abraham, Isaac, and of Israel, let it be known this day that thou art God in Israel,
and that I am thy servant, and that I have done all these things at thy word.
37 Hear me, O Lord, hear me, that this people may know that thou art the Lord God, and that thou hast turned their heart back again.
38 Then the fire of the Lord fell, and consumed the burnt sacrifice, and the wood, and the stones, and the dust, and licked up the water that was in the trench.

39 And when all the people saw it, they fell on their faces: and they said, The Lord, he is the God; the Lord, he is the God.

Now the Bible teaches the effectual fervent prayer of a righteous man accomplishes much. How did Elijah prayer an effectual prayer? Notice how Elijah had to pray in the will of God by great exertion in intercessory prayer. Even though Elijah knew God wanted to end the three years of drought, Elijah had to pray through the will of God with great effort. Elijah fell down on His knees with His face to the ground to pray for rain. Elijah cast himself down great urgency standing as an intercessor between God and Israel.

Often in prevailing prayer a continuance is required until a breakthrough. Elijah was a man, a servant of the Lord who had stood in the council of the Lord and stood on behalf of Israel. Seven times in prevailing prayer Elijah made intercession for Israel. I find it amazing Elijah had just seen the miracle of Fire falling from heaven in answer to his sacrifice and prayer. Now Elijah must prevail with God on his knees seven times crying out to God for His will to be done, and to end the three years of Gods judgment of drought. Elijah must prevail with God as a righteous man with effectual prayer asking God as an intercessor. Finally, a small cloud the size of a man's hand appeared, and Elijah knew God had answered before anyone else did. Elijah's life is characteristic of the life of Jesus Christ. Herein is the true answer to praying in the Spirit. A man who will truly follow the Lord as his servant putting others first will be a man of prayer. Not only a man of prayer, but a man whose prayers move heaven.

1 Kings 18:42-44
42 So Ahab went up to eat and to drink. And Elijah went up to the top of Carmel; and he cast himself down upon the earth, and put his face between his knees,
43 And said to his servant, Go up now, look toward the sea. And he went up, and looked, and said, There is nothing. And he said, Go again seven times.
44 And it came to pass at the seventh time, that he said, Behold, there ariseth a little cloud out of the sea, like a man's hand. And he said, Go up, say unto Ahab, Prepare thy chariot, and get thee down, that the rain stop thee not.

Chapter Nine
The Holy Spirit and Manifest Presence of God

On the Day of Pentecost, the Holy Spirit suddenly descended into the Upper Room where over one hundred saints were waiting. Even though the Holy Spirit is the third person of the Godhead, the Holy Spirit manifested that day as "wind and fire" before filling the saints with the Baptism of the Holy Spirit. The manifest presence of God does happen from time to time and can be experienced in a very real and tangible way. Here in lies the danger in the Charismatic Movement, as

Christians can get caught up with seeking experiences of the supernatural and fall into the error of yielding to demonic spirits. No where in the Scriptures are Christians instructed to "seek manifestations," instead we are to seek God Himself.

Hebrews 11:6

[6] But without faith it is impossible to please him: for he, that cometh to God must believe that he is, and that he is a rewarder of them that diligently seek him.

So much of the walk of faith is without any sensuous experiences, without any God feelings, or experiences of the supernatural of any kind. Often the Christian must deny his own feelings, or circumstances and pick up the Cross to follow the Lord. When the walk of faith requires self-denial and can often feel as if the Lord is far away. Therefore, Charismatics often seduce Christians with the promises of supernatural experiences, as it gives "instant gratification to the flesh." Sadly, when young Christians came to think "getting drunk in the spirit," is about experiencing God, and keep going to meetings to get their next high or drunken feelings. After they leave their schools of the supernatural often, they fall into disillusionment as most Churches are not about "getting drunk in the spirit," or having experiences. Its almost become a spiritual addiction instead of drugs or alcohol the addiction is now mood altering by getting drunk spirituality. Is this drunkenness the result of the presence of the Holy Spirit? It is definitely not when the same thing is "acted out by Christian's meeting after meeting."

The manifest presence of God has a very redemptive purpose. Can a Charismatic leader experience his body burning with supernatural sensations coming upon him when seeking experiences from God? Yes and no. Sometime the Holy Spirit will manifest in feelings of fire or heat like on the Day of Pentecost. However, I know about the testimony of a self-declared apostle who said he was "electrocuted" by the presence of God. He said electrical currents of the supernatural surged through his body immobilizing on the ground for many minutes. From that time, this same apostle has brough forth false doctrines on signs and wonders. Everything has become about bringing supernatural experiences from heaven to earth.

Was his electrocution the result of the manifest presence of God? Absolutely not? Its fruit led him to preach against the divinity of Jesus in the Incarnation, so every Charismatic could have "power and manifestations just like Jesus." False doctrine and heresy have followed his supernatural experience. Why, an evil spirit, an angel of light has deceived this self-declared apostle to believe being electrocuted is "the power of God?" Instead, it was an "imitation of the Holy

Spirit" in false and sensuous supernatural manifestations. Ever since, this same false apostle has taught Charismatics to recover the New Age which he says has been stole from the Church.

A whole Charismatic Movement has come under the influences of New Age phenomena, as the result of a man being electrocuted by supernatural presence which he thought was the manifest presence of God. Instead, the Holy Spirit would never lead men into supernatural experiences which pull them away from the Scriptures and walking in the Spirit of Truth. Evil spirits imitating the manifest presence of God have invaded the Signs and Wonders Charismatic Movement.

2 Corinthians 11:12-20
[12] But what I do, that I will do, that I may cut off occasion from them which desire occasion; that wherein they glory, they may be found even as we.
[13] For such are false apostles, deceitful workers, transforming themselves into the apostles of
Christ.
[14] And no marvel; for Satan himself is transformed into an angel of light.
[15] Therefore it is no great thing if his ministers also be transformed as the ministers of righteousness; whose end shall be according to their works.
[16] I say again, let no man think me a fool; if otherwise, yet as a fool receive me, that I may boast myself a little.

¹⁷ That which I speak, I speak it not after the Lord, but as it were foolishly, in this confidence of boasting.

¹⁸ Seeing that many glory after the flesh, I will glory also.

¹⁹ For ye suffer fools gladly, seeing ye yourselves are wise.

²⁰ For ye suffer, if a man bring you into bondage, if a man devour you, if a man take of you, if a man exalt himself, if a man smite you on the face.

The Holy Spirit Is a Person, Not an Atmosphere

Perhaps the lack of holding the Holy Spirit as a person has hurt the Charismatic as any other deception. The Bible never describes the Holy Spirit as an "atmosphere," or an impersonal force, or something supernatural which is independent of the person of the Holy Spirit. What happens on a supernatural basis in the Christian faith comes from the person of the Holy Spirit, even when displays of power or gifts are manifested. All miracles, signs, and wonders in the Christian faith come from the person of the Holy Spirit. No healings, miracles, prophecy, come independently by a ministry, instead are a direct result of the person of the Holy Spirit. Why does the Scriptures call the gifts, the gifts of the Holy Spirit? The gifts of the Holy Spirit come from the person of the Holy Spirit and are not owned by a person who manifests them. Notice the language, now the manifestation of the Spirit is given to every man to profit with all. The gifts of the Holy Spirit manifest by the Person of the Holy Spirit even when being worked through a Christian. Keeping with the Holy Spirit as a person, not just any common person instead the third person in the Godhead. Father, Son, and the Holy Spirit are coequal, coeternal, and consubstantial, are the three persons of the one and only uncreated God. That's why the Holy Spirit is called the Spirit of God.

Now the Spirit of God indwells the born-again Christian by the Holy Spirit. Do you see how the Scriptures emphasize the Holy Spirit when it comes to working the gifts? It is never said to create an atmosphere or look for a supernatural force to move upon you. Instead, the Holy Spirit chooses by His own will and purpose who and when to manifest any of the gifts. The dependance is up the person of the Holy Spirit, and not some atmospheric change which makes for the "god feeling." Why is this distinction important? As the Holy Spirit is not limited to "environments, or atmospheres, or people's feelings or sense about the "god feeling." As the Spirit of God works with Christians who are walking in the Spirit no matter how dark, or evil, or demonic in the situation. God does not need to "develop a sensuous atmosphere" in order to manifest the gifts of the Holy Spirit. As man is not in control of the Holy Spirit but can "resist the Holy Spirit by unbelief."

Notice these facts when it comes to the gifts of the Holy Spirit. 1) No man can say Jesus Christ is Lord but by the Holy Spirit. Meaning authentic prophecy comes from the Holy Spirit, and no man can independently of the Holy Spirits leading a give a "true prophetic word." A great problem has arisen in the Charismatic Movement as men speak by their own wills, and without the leading of the Holy Spirit. In plain simple language these false prophets refuse to follow God the Holy Spirit.

God the Holy Spirit chooses the time, the way, the person by which the gifts of the Holy Spirit will function. The Scriptures says the administration of the gifts is by the Person of the Holy Spirit. Also, the gifts operations are by the same God (Holy Spirit), and no man can choose to make God manifest, as there is no such operation in the Christian faith as "gifts upon demand." That's why so much corruption has come through the denial of the Holy Spirit as a person, and His will. No Christian can have visions upon demand, or prophecy, or miracles, or trips into heaven. Even though this has become common practice inside the Prophetic Charismatic Movement it's a violation of the will and Person of God.

What is happening then when Christians experience the supernatural upon demand and its not coming from the leading of the Holy Spirit. The answer lies in the power of the mystical, and the New Age. As those manifestations come from the "mans soul power," like psychic powers, and fortune telling." It can even come from evil spirits like lying dreams, visions, and angels of light. Evil spirts, fallen angels, angels of light which imitate the person of God. Leading those whom they deceive away from following the Holy Spirit and working lying signs and wonders by tempting Christians to manifest the supernatural independent of the Holy Spirit.

1 Corinthians 12:1-7

Now concerning spiritual gifts, brethren, I would not have you ignorant.

[2] Ye know that ye were Gentiles, carried away unto these dumb idols, even as ye were led.

[3] Wherefore I give you to understand, that no man speaking by the Spirit of God calleth Jesus accursed: and that no man can say that Jesus is the Lord, but by the Holy Ghost.

[4] Now there are diversities of gifts, but the same Spirit.

[5] And there are differences of administrations, but the same Lord.

[6] And there are diversities of operations, but it is the same God which worketh all in all.

[7] But the manifestation of the Spirit is given to every man to profit withal.

Chapter Ten

The Holy Spirit and Fruit of the Spirit

When Charismatics speak of the Holy Spirit the subject is usually related to the power of the Holy Spirit. In this case the Holy Spirit is about the power to be a witness, so the work of the Spirit is from your life towards others. Some good examples would be the Gifts of the Holy Spirit which manifest in healings or deliverance which are displays of Gods power. However, a another very important aspect of the Holy Spirit is the indwelling presence in believers which then bring forth the nature and character of Jesus Christ. Part of this growth and development is called the "fruit of the Spirit."

Galatians 5:22
22 But the fruit of the Spirit is love, joy, peace, long suffering, gentleness, goodness, faith,
23 Meekness, temperance: against such there is no law.

Notice what the fruit of the Spirit grows inside our lives as we walk in the Spirit and grow up into greater Christlikeness. The first fruit listed is love which is also of supreme importance, as the first two commandments of Jesus Christ are love commandments. Walking in love is to walk-in the Spirit as compared to walking in the flesh and serving your own self interests. With the Fruit of the Spirit, we learn to grow in grace, and love becomes one of the primary ways we express the nature of Jesus Christ through our lives. Of course, the love of God often proves to be very different than natural human love, as we commonly love those who love us, but Jesus Christ teaches His disciples to love their enemies. Without the presence of the Holy Spirit making for the fruit of love your natural human tendencies will react in defense, as only the love of God could help you turn the other cheek while suffering in the love of God.

The fruit of the Spirit has qualities which natural human abilities falls short. For example, having the joy of the Lord in the face of suffering. Only God could supply the fruit of long suffering coupled with joy when facing circumstances which require suffering. These are qualities which come from God Himself and can grow and develop in the lives of the saints as the fruit of the Spirit. Jesus Christ Himself was meek and lowly of heart which demonstrates the character and nature of God, who when He was reviled, He reviled not. Like a Lamb being led to slaughter we esteemed Him stricken and smitten of God, but surely, He bore our grief and carried our sorrows. The fruit of the Spirit shows us the nature and charter of Jesus Christ in our lives when we follow the Lord submitting our wills to the will of the Lord.

Notice there is no laws made which says a man has "too much love, or too much forgiveness, who lives his life in peace with his neighbor. Against the fruit of the Spirit there is no law, as it contrasts with the character and fruit of the world. The world does not know peace, yet the fruit of the Holy Spirit gives us the peace of God which passes understanding guarding our hearts and minds. As the world continues to grow in fear, anxiety of mind and sorrow of heart, the fruit of sowing and reaping of sin. As lawless abounds the saints must stand with the Holy Spirit demonstrating the fruit of the Spirit in the face of growing darkness. While the world falls to the spirit of antichrist, those who have "fruit" from the Holy Spirit will reprove the world of sin, righteous, and judgment simply by living right before God. The fruit of faith shines brightly in the midst of gross darkness.

Why all the falling away from the faith in our day? As all the sensuous experiences give way to the growing darkness and the difficulty of the fiery trials of our faith. Men who have "no fruit will wilt," as the glory of man is as the grass which withers in the face of draught. While those who walk in the Spirit and have grown up in the Lord, will feast on the fruit of the Spirit in the face of a lost and dying world.

The Holy Spirit and the Divine Nature

When the Bible speaks of Christians partaking in the "Divine Nature," it does not mean a born-again Christian is a divine person or becoming a divine person. One of the huge heretical teachings of the 7 Mountain New Apostolic Reformation is to make a "divine man out of Christians, or fulling up the Church with the divinity of God. The difference of partaking of the divine nature, and being a divine person are separated by an "infinity."

To put it simply or frankly, man born again and partaking of the divine nature is not becoming God, a god, or a divine man. The divine nature is a "nature unto itself," and can never be created or reproduced. There is no such person as a "God Man," except found in the one only Begotten Son of God. Jesus Christ in the Incarnation is fully God and fully Man, the one and only divine man who will have ever existed throughout all eternity.

How then do born again Christians partake of the divine nature, without becoming a divine man? Here is the Scriptural explanation which teaches how we partake of the divine nature.

2 Peter 1:4

[4] Whereby are given unto us exceeding great and precious promises: that by these ye might be partakers of the divine nature, having escaped the corruption that is in the world through lust.

God made promise mankind could escape the fallen world by sin and death by partaking of the divine nature, which was given when Christians receive salvation by grace through faith in Christ. When a man is born again, the incorruptible seed is planted on the inside making the fallen nature of the human spirit transformed by the life of Christ. The incorruptible seed gives the new nature, old things have passed away, and all things have become new. Not a new God man instead a new man in Christ designated a born-again son of God. Always a man, but now indwelt by the Spirit of God, a born-again man partaking of the incorruptible seed the Word of God that lives and abides forever. The divine nature is from God, Jesus Christ, the Word of God, and the Spirit of God indwelling in us. Our human spirit is transformed from slavery to sin into a born-again human spirit with the life of Christ. Our human spirit remains a human spirit, not a divine spirit, however, has been transformed by the Spirit of God indwelling us when we come to faith in Christ.

When apostles of the 7 Mountain NAR teach Charismatics there are divine, or are becoming divine, or filling up with divinity its pure unadulterated heresy. What we see in this heresy making Christians into the exact measure of divinity as found in Jesus Christ. The bridge of infinity exists between Jesus Christ and His creation including every man, woman, and child. Never can the bridge of the uncreated God be spanned by any of His creation where man becomes God without any limitations. Omnipresent, Omnipotent, and Omniscient never are these qualities ever to be found in mankind throughout all eternity. Only the New Age, Occult, and religions outside the Christian faith attempt to make a "divine man, a God, or God." How perverse when self-proclaimed apostles teach the Church is in the process of becoming a divine man.

Being born again and indwelt by the Holy Spirit does not make a man just like Jesus. Instead, we partake of the divine nature supplied by Jesus Christ through the indwelling presence of the Spirit of Christ. A true separation between Gods divinity, and our humanity continues even though we partake of the Life of Christ, called eternal life. That part which continues without sin inside of us is the Incorruptible Seed the Life of Christ the Word of God, however though we are born again with a new nature we are still capable of living after the flesh. While Christs life is one completely sinless.

1 John 3:1-10
Behold, what manner of love the Father hath bestowed upon us, that we should be called the sons of God: therefore, the world knoweth us not, because it knew him not.

2 Beloved, now are we the sons of God, and it doth not yet appear what we shall be: but we know that, when he shall appear, we shall be like him; for we shall see him as he is.
3 And every man that hath this hope in him purifieth himself, even as he is pure.
4 Whosoever committeth sin transgresseth also the law: for sin is the transgression of the law.
5 And ye know that he was manifested to take away our sins; and in him is no sin.
6 Whosoever abideth in him sinneth not: whosoever sinneth hath not seen him, neither known him.

[7] Little children, let no man deceive you: he that doeth righteousness is righteous, even as he is
righteous.
[8] He that committeth sin is of the devil; for the devil sinneth from the beginning.
For this purpose, the Son of God was manifested, that he might destroy the works of the devil.
[9] Whosoever is born of God doth not commit sin; for his seed remaineth in him: and he cannot sin, because he is born of God.
[10] In this the children of God are manifest, and the children of the devil: whosoever doeth not righteousness is not of God, neither he that loveth not his brother.

Chapter Eleven
Work of the Holy Spirit

The Christian faith is salvation from sin, the fallen world, Satan and Kingdom of Darkness, and death. We often see how the Cross of Jesus Christ has given us "redemption through His Blood," our position before God is justified, holy, blameless, without reproof if we continue in the faith. Often Christians don't see the intricate connection with the Cross, and the work of the Holy Spirit. Often the teaching of the acts of the Holy Spirit is about manifestations, and experiences. What often is neglected is how the Holy Spirit is intricately connected to the Cross and will not act outside what the Cross has provided in our redemption. Attempting to make the Holy Spirit a work unto Himself is not the record of Scriptures, as the Holy Spirit does not highlight Himself instead is all about lifting Jesus Christ. The Church blows up when it is all about the Holy Spirit, and the Cross is left out. When the Holy Spirit is working it is all about Jesus Christ, to worship the Lord in Spirit and in Truth.

Here are three major works of the Holy Spirit which are ever present when the Holy Spirit is revealing Jesus Christ and the Redemption of the Cross. The work of the Holy Spirit would 1) Reprove the world of sin, or "conviction of sin." 2) Conviction of the righteousness of God in Christ and 3) Judgment of a man's condition before God, the result of redeeming man from sin, death, Satan, and eternal damnation. Satan and this fallen world has been judged and appointed for the fire of Gods wrath.

Once a man comes into saving grace, the Holy Spirit will continue to speak and show us the truth that is found in Jesus Christ alone. As mankind must have a revelation of Jesus Christ in order to come into saving faith, the work of the Holy Spirit will just "deepen" those truths found in Jesus Christ alone. He shall not speak of Himself, but whatsoever He (Holy Spirit) hears from Jesus Christ the Head of the Church, He (Holy Spirit) will speak, and show it unto the Church.

The Holy Spirit is not "looking to add new revelations" to what Jesus Christ has already taught and spoken. Instead, will only show and build upon what has already been given. What makes the written Word of God given by the inspiration of the Holy Spirit, and is the eternal, infallible, incorruptible Word of God. How dangerous is the practice of Christians to add or subtract from what the Word of God has already given? The Holy Spirit is not "giving new light of revelations" which have never before been given, and apart from what has already been written in the Scriptures. How dangerous and deceptive to attach the name of the Holy Spirit when a self-declared prophets say God has shown me, or God has told me, or I went into heaven, and their prophetic word violates what has already been written in Scriptures. How simply would evil spirits have been exposed, and false prophets, if Christians would "test the spirits by the written Word of God." As the Holy Spirit will never work outside the bounds of the Written Word of God.

John 16:7-
15

[7] Nevertheless I tell you the truth; It is expedient for you that I go away: for if I go not away, the Comforter will not come unto you; but if I depart, I will send him unto you.

[8] And when he is come, he will reprove the world of sin, and of righteousness, and of judgment:

9 Of sin, because they believe not on me;

10 Of righteousness, because I go to my Father, and ye see me no more;

11 Of judgment, because the prince of this world is judged.

12 I have yet many things to say unto you, but ye cannot bear them now.

13 Howbeit when he, the Spirit of truth, is come, he will guide you into all truth: for he shall not speak of himself; but whatsoever he shall hear, that shall he speak: and he will shew you things to come.

14 He shall glorify me: for he shall receive of mine and shall shew it unto you.

15 All things that the Father hath are mine: therefore, said I, that he shall take of mine, and shall shew it unto you

The Holy Spirit as the Anointing

In the Old Testament book of Isaiah, we have been given a description of the anointing of Jesus Christ for the work of ministry. The Holy Spirit anointed Jesus Christ with the ability to preach, and do works of the Spirit in healing, miracles, and deliverance. The Hebrew word for "anointed" is "Mashach" meaning to consecrate, to set apart for the work. In this case Jesus Christ was anointed with the Holy Spirit without measure, while all others anointed by the Holy Spirit will be by measure.

Isaiah 61:1-3

1 The Spirit of the Lord God is upon me; because the Lord hath anointed me to preach good tidings unto the meek; he hath sent me to bind up the brokenhearted, to proclaim liberty to the captives, and the opening of the prison to them that are bound;
2 To proclaim the acceptable year of the Lord, and the day of vengeance of our God; to comfort all that mourn;
3 To appoint unto them that mourn in Zion, to give unto them beauty for ashes, the oil of joy for mourning, the garment of praise for the spirit of heaviness; that they might be called trees of righteousness, the planting of the Lord, that he might be glorified.

As the Lord was anointed by the Holy Spirit, the Scriptures point out Christ was to preach good tidings to the meek. Also, Jesus would bring healing to the broken hearted, to set those free held captive by sin and evil spirits. To proclaim God's forgiveness and salvation, to give beauty for ashes, and praise in place of depression and sorrow. The Lord would bring forth a mighty harvest of sons and daughters of God by the work of the Cross and Resurrection. Finally, to declare the coming Kingdom of Heaven age, and the vengeance of our God.

In a similar way God gives the Holy Spirit anointing to every member of the body of Christ to fulfill a work given by God. The anointing given to the members of the Church Universal is by measure according to the work the Lord has called each member to fulfill. When a

Christian is born again, they have received eternal life in Christ, and in answering the call to service the Holy Spirit then empowers them for the work of service. The anointing is placed upon each person by the Holy Spirit painting or applying a measure for each person's calling.

In ministry callings each person has been given a unique portion of the Holy Spirits anointing. Each one called of the Lord must choose to answer the call before they can see the Lords anointing upon their lives. When a person walks in agreement to the call of God you will see the divine enablement which allows them to minister according to Gods anointing upon their lives. That is why we see many who are called to preach who are not necessarily educated or experts but have been given an ability beyond these natural abilities. Jesus Christ chooses uneducated fishermen who by the anointing were able to shake the world with the Gospel of Jesus Christ.

At the baptism of Jesus Christ, the Holy Spirit descended upon Him in the form of a dove. After which Jesus Christ went into the wilderness too fast for forty days, and after was tempted of the devil. When Jesus Christ defeated the Satan's temptations, He came back to Nazareth to declare the start of His ministry. At this point Jesus Christ quoted Isaiah Jesus Christ said He was the fulfillment of Isaiah's prophecy being the Christos, the anointed. However, the people of Nazareth refused the testimony of Jesus Christ, and took him to the brow of the hill and push Jesus Christ to death for declaring He was the Christ.

Which demonstrates the cost of the anointing? When answering the call of God upon your life every person must understand there is a price to walk in the anointing. The cost upon the person's life can be seen in personal loss, while at the same time the fruitfulness for the Lord can bring the Lord glory. Here is an example of the cost of the anointing by the apostle Peter who was so anointed by the Holy Spirit for miracles that even the shadow of Peter could cause those who needed a miracle to walk or be restored to health as Peters shadow touched them when he walked by.

Acts 5:12-16
12 And by the hands of the
apostles were many signs and wonders wrought
among the people; (and they all with one
accord in Solomon's porch.
13 And of the rest durst no man join himself to
them: but the people magnified them.
14 And believers were the more added to the
Lord, multitudes both of men and women.)
15 Insomuch that they brought forth the sick into the
streets, and laid them on beds and couches, that at the
shadow of Peter passing by might overshadow some of
them.
16 There came also a multitude out of the cities round
about unto Jerusalem, bringing sick folks, and

them which were vexed with unclean spirits: and they were healed everyone.

However, we must remember the cost upon Peters life to walk in the miracle anointing of the Lord. As Jesus Christ warned Peter Satan sought to sift the faith of Peter where he would deny the Lord three times before the rooster would crow. Peter's failure drove him out of the ministry back into the fishing business which Peter had to surrender to follow the Lord. Afterwards the Lord would recover the ministry of Peter, and Peter was the principal preacher on the Day of Pentecost.
After Peter began to preach and work miracles through the anointing upon His life. Which resulted in sufferings and even imprisonment. Peter would demonstrate Jesus Christ was in fact raised from the dead working miracles in Jesus Christ name. After which the religious leaders would attack Peter putting him in prison simply for working a miracle by the Holy Spirit anointing.
No man should take lightly the cost which has been paid by the saints over the Church age to fulfill the call and anointing upon the saints. Each person must be willing to pick up the Cross in self-denial and follow the Lord in the fellowship of Christs sufferings. If you choose to walk in the call upon your life, you too will pay the price of the anointing.

Acts 5:17-33

17 Then the high priest rose up, and all they that
were with him, (which is the sect of the Sadducees,) and
were filled with indignation,
18 And laid their hands on the
apostles, and put them in the common prison.
19 But the angel of the Lord by night opened the
prison doors, and brought them forth, and said,
20 Go, stand and speak in the temple to the
people all the words of this life.
21 And when they heard that, they entered into the
temple early in the morning, and taught. But the high
priest came, and they that
were with him, and called the
council together, and all the senate of the children of
Israel, and sent to the prison to have them brought.
22 But when the
officers came, and found them not in the prison, they
returned, and told,
23 Saying, The prison truly found
we shut with all safety, and the
keepers standing without before the doors: but when
we had opened, we found no man within.
24 Now when the high priest and the captain of the
temple and the chief priests heard these things, they
doubted of them whereunto this would grow.
25 Then came one and told them, saying, Behold, the
men whom ye put in prison are standing in the
temple, and teaching the people.
26 Then went the captain with the
officers, and brought them without violence: for they

feared the people, lest they should have been stoned.
27 And when they had brought them, they
set them before the council: and the high priest asked
them,
28 Saying, Did not we straitly command you that ye
should not teach in this name? and, behold, ye have
filled Jerusalem with your doctrine, and intend to
bring this man's blood upon us.
29 Then Peter and the other apostles answered and said
, We ought to obey God rather than men.
30 The God of our fathers raised
up Jesus, whom ye slew and hanged on a tree.
31 Him hath God exalted with his right hand to be a
Prince and a Saviour, for to give repentance to
Israel, and forgiveness of sins.
32 And we are his witnesses of these things; and so
is also the Holy Ghost, whom God hath given to
them that obey him.
33 When they heard that, they were cut to the
heart, and took counsel to slay them.

The Holy Spirit and Conviction

One of the most overlooked aspects of the Holy Spirit is
conviction of sin. In the modern organized Church,
anything to stop offense at religion has created an
atmosphere of no confrontation of sin. The feel-good
religion of today allows a man to sit in a religious service
living in immorality and feel strong emotion like love,
and peace without having to "repent of an immoral life

of sin." However, a man can die in his sins separated from God and face the wrath of God in eternal judgment. A man can have the God feeling and die under the judgment of God to face Hell, and then the Lake of Fire.

How can we discern the absence of God? Not by feelings, or spiritual highs, or emoting to worship music, instead the Holy Spirit will bring conviction to our commitment to the Lordship of Jesus Christ. Will God be pleased with a life of sin? Will God allow a life or self will and rebellion? Will a man be allowed into heaven in the state of rebellion even when He is a member in good standing inside the Church? When a man truly walks with God, truly walks in the Spirit, he must deny himself and pick up the Cross to follow Jesus Christ. Any man who is living for the Lord will be "convicted by the Holy Spirit," when anything done is an offense to the Lord. This aspect of "grieving the Holy Spirit," is the result of doing something outside of the will of God.

Why all the fake revivals of today, why all the false doctrines and practices? Is heaven coming to earth and making the world Christian? A Church which declares the "goodness of man" which speaks to spiritual dead men a prophetic word, "saying thus says the Lord you have a great destiny in God." Will God speak to a man dead in sin, in rebellion to God all is well with your life and future? This practice comes from the Antichrist

Spirit and is a complete suppression of the Gospel of Salvation the Cross of Jesus Christ. A false Gospel called the Kingdom of God has invaded the pulpits of the Charismatic Movement which declares there is no "future judgment, only a golden age remains for the earth." As the world is full of sin displayed in hate, rebellion, bloodshed, a total denial of sin and death must be kept out of the pulpits. Anyone who speaks of the coming wrath of God is called a "prophet of doom," and declared a religious pharisee.

Where is the Holy Spirit the Spirit of Truth who convicts the world of sin, and of righteousness and of judgment? The cost of following the Holy Spirit is not spoken in modern theology as the Holy Spirit has been made a puppet to man's selfish demands. Look at the practice of declaring visions upon demand, visitations in heaven upon demand. It looks like the Holy Spirit is subjected to the demands of the Charismatic Church. The truth told, the Holy Spirit does nothing to lift up a man into self-glorification, the Holy Spirit is never given to enable the flesh of man. What spirit is giving man all the supernatural manifestations they lust for upon demand? A lying spirit, a spirit of error, who wants to appeal to the flesh of man imitating the presence of God. Satan is the Prince of the Power of the Air the spirit which has led the heavens and earth in rebellion to God.

Why is the Holy Spirit called Holy when holiness is being suppressed in the Church? Why is He called the Spirit of Truth when lies and deception have become what is called "the truth?" Why is there so much of a "god feeling," when sin and rebellion are left without a word of confrontation? The only real answer is this is not the work of the Holy Spirit. When the Holy Spirit functions in true conviction no man can have peace living in sin, and in rebellion to God. No man likes to come "under the conviction of guilt," and would want to run and hide from a Holy God. The only relief would be found in the Blood of the Lamb, a true confession of sin, and a trusting in the Cross for the payment of our guilt and debt to sin. A saint walking with the Lord in the Spirit is become very familiar with the dealings of the Holy Spirit. Conviction of sin, the flesh, and death t love of the world comes from the work of the Holy Spirit. Without the "Spirit of Grace," no man can escape the constant presence of sin and death. A man who walks with God in the Spirit has become familiar with the Holy Spirits conviction and call to surrender to the Cross.

John 16:7-14

7 Nevertheless I tell you the truth; It is expedient for you that I go away: for if I go not away, the Comforter will not come unto you; but if I depart, I will send him unto you.

8 And when he is come, he will reprove the world of sin, and of righteousness, and of judgment:

⁹ Of sin, because they believe not on me;

¹⁰ Of righteousness, because I go to my Father, and ye see me no more;

¹¹ Of judgment, because the prince of this world is judged.

¹² I have yet many things to say unto you, but ye cannot bear them now.

¹³ Howbeit when he, the Spirit of truth, is come, he will guide you into all truth: for he shall not speak of himself; but whatsoever he shall hear, that shall he speak: and he will shew you things to come.

¹⁴ He shall glorify me: for he shall receive of mine and shall shew it unto you.

Part III
Testing the Spirit

Chapter Twelve
The Holy Spirit as Spirit of Prophecy

In Prophetic Ministry the Holy Spirit is also called the Testimony of Jesus the Spirit of Prophecy. Which is related to Gods infallible words, as recorded in the prophetic words of Scriptures. As all Scriptures are given by inspiration God and are the Word of God which cannot fail or lie. One great example is in the Book of Revelation where the apostle John is given visions about the Second Coming of Jesus Christ, and the end time of Gods judgments in age ending events. At one point the apostle John is so overwhelmed by these visions, he falls to exalt one of the heavenly elders. At which the heavenly elder corrects John's actions, saying the revelations are the result of the Holy Spirit as the Testimony of Jesus the Spirit of Prophecy.

Revelation 19:10
10 And I fell at his feet to worship him. And he said unto me, See thou do it not: I am thy fellow servant, and of thy brethren that have the testimony of
Jesus: worship God: for the testimony of Jesus is the spirit of prophecy.

Real "revelations" from the Holy Spirit will always exalt the person of Jesus Christ and bring the Lord His glory. The Lord by the Holy Spirit raised up His holy apostles and prophets to lay the foundation of the Prophetic Words recorded in Scriptures as the infallible Word of God. Here is an example of the infallible revelations of the Holy Spirit as described by the apostle Peter when Jesus Christ took Peter, John, and James upon the Holy Mountain. Where these men saw by vision the Transformation of Jesus Christ, along with the appearing of Moses and Elijah. Where upon Peter heard the infallible voice of God declaring Jesus Christ to be the eternal Son of God. Peter speaks of this prophetic vision in his letter to the Churches and its infallible revelation of Jesus Christ.

Peter says the prophetic revelations given by the Holy Spirit to the apostles and prophets of old should not be treated as tales designed to deceive mankind. As Peter says they are eyes witness of not only Christs resurrection, but the majesty declared by God of Jesus Christ upon the Holy Mount. Peter said the vision is the infallible word of God, and its declaration of Jesus Christ as Gods Son.

Now, Peter honors this Holy Spirit revelation as the more sure word of Prophecy making this vision an instrumental promise given by the Spirit of Prophecy. Since this word of Prophecy is now the infallible word of God, anyone who has heard of this prophetic vision should take heed until the Lord Jesus Christ returns to make good the promise of the coming Kingdom age which was shown Peter and the other apostles upon the Holy Mount. As the day dawns overthrowing the darkness of this present evil age, and the Day Star appears by the resurrection of the dead in Christ and saints of old.

Peter, then warns these Holy Spirit revelations are to be counted as the infallible words of God, and not from a man's private revelations. The apostles and prophets of old were given these prophetic words and visions as Gods future promises. To war a good warfare of faith when this present evil age rejects the word of God and refuses the revelation of Jesus Christ. As these Holy Spirit words of Prophecy were given by holy men and Christs apostles who saw and wrote the infallible words of prophetic revelation.

2 Peter 1:16-21.
16 For we have not followed cunningly
devised fables, when we made known unto you the
power andcoming of our Lord Jesus Christ, but were eye
witnesses of his majesty.
17 For he received from God the
Father honour and glory, when there came such a
voice to
him fromthe excellent glory, This is my beloved Son, in
whom I am well pleased.
18 And this voice which
came from heaven we heard, when we
were with him in the holy mount.
19 We have also a more sure word of
prophecy; whereunto ye do well that ye take heed, as
unto a light that shineth in a dark place, until the
day dawn, and the day star arise in your hearts:
20 Knowing this first, that no prophecy of the
scripture is of any private interpretation.
21 For the prophecy came not in old time by the will of
man: but holy men of God spake as they were moved by
the Holy Ghost.

The apostle Peter exhorts the Church to receive the
prophetic words given by the prophets of old as those
who laid a foundation of Gods infallible word. Peter
teaches the trials of our faith are a war against the
promises of God, and we are to fight a good fight of
faith laying hold of what God has said through His holy

apostles and prophets. Though you have not seen the Lord you love, yet not seeing him you believe receiving the end of your faith even the salvation of your souls. Of which we wage a good warfare holding fast the promises found in the written Word of God. Of this salvation the prophets of old spoke by the inspiration of the Holy Spirit of the grace which shall come unto you. They we are searching for the time and manner the Lord would manifest His sufferings and glory which should follow. Now these prophetic promises are being fulfilled, and at the coming of the Lord, and by the Holy Spirit sent from heaven on the day of Pentecost. Of these things given by Gods prophetic word even the angels of the Lord desire to look into. Hold fast the promises of God at the revelation of Jesus Christ is our future hope and walk of faith.

1 Peter 1:7-13
7 That the trial of your faith, being much more precious than of gold that perisheth, though it be tried
with fire, might be
found unto praise and honour and glory at the appearing of Jesus Christ:
8 Whom having not seen, ye love; in whom, though now ye see him not, yet believing, ye rejoice with joy unspeakable and full of glory:
9 Receiving the end of your faith, even the salvation of your souls.
10 Of which salvation the prophets have enquired and searched diligently, who

prophesied of the grace that should come unto you:
11 Searching what, or what manner of time the Spirit of
Christ which was in them did signify, when it
testified beforehand the sufferings of Christ, and the
glory that should follow.
12 Unto whom it was revealed, that not unto
themselves, but unto us they did minister the
things, which are now reported unto you by them that
have preached the gospel unto you with the Holy Ghost
sent from heaven; which things the angels desire to
look into.
13 Wherefore gird up the loins of your mind, be
sober, and hope to the end for the grace that is to be
brought unto you at the revelation of Jesus Christ;

Prophetic words given by the Scriptures have come by
the Spirit of Prophecy and are the infallible word of
God. As compared to the New Testament gift of
Prophecy which must be judged and tested for its
accuracy. For New Testament words of prophecy also
come by inspiration of the Holy Spirit but are not the
infallible word of God. Which makes New Testament
prophetic words subject to what has already been
written in Scriptures. All New Testament prophecy must
be tested for private interpretations and subjective
revelations done in the name of the Lord but violate the
written word of God.

Chapter Thirteen
Holy Spirit Dreams and Visions

In both the Old and New Testaments dreams and visions are an instrumental part of Gods revelations among his people. Here is an example of a New Testament vision given to the apostle Peter as recorded in the Book of Acts.

Acts 10:9-16

9 On the morrow, as they went on their journey, and drew nigh unto the city, Peter went up upon the housetop to pray about the sixth hour:

10 And he became very hungry, and would have eaten: but while they made ready, he fell into a trance,

11 And saw heaven opened, and a certain vessel descending unto him, as it had been a great sheet knit at the four corners, and let down to the earth:

12 Wherein were all manner of four footed beasts of the earth, and wild beasts, and creeping things, and fowls of the air.

13 And there came a voice to him, Rise, Peter; kill, and eat.

14 But Peter said, Not so, Lord; for I have never eaten any thing that is common or unclean.

15 And the voice spake unto him again the second time, What God hath cleansed, that call not thou common.

16 This was done thrice: and the vessel was received up again into heaven.

Peter had a trance vision given by the Holy Spirit to lead and guide Peter into the Lords will. What is a trance vision? Peter fell into a trance where his natural senses were suspended so he could see by vision the images which God wanted to display. These images appeared as if Peter could see with his own natural eyes. They appeared as if Peter was seeing them right there in his prayer room, but, was a vision which appeared as real as anything in the room. A trance vision is just one of the highest measures of visions as the senses of the person are being influenced by the Holy Spirit.

Another highly advanced vision given by the Holy Spirit is called an open vision. In this case, the persons ability to see what is normally hidden to the natural eyes are now enabled to see into the Spirit what was before unable to be seen by the natural senses. Sometimes in open visions Christians have been given the ability to see and converse with Jesus Christ, and even Gods angels. One thing is certain, visions given by God coming from the Holy Spirit are not under the control of man. No man can upon his own will and demand make for the visions of God.

Peter's trance vision came ten years after the Day of Pentecost. While the Jews who had come to faith at Pentecost had yet to spread the message to the Gentiles. As the Jewish bellves still held to the practice of Old Testament law where Jews considered interactions with the Gentiles would make them ceremonially unclean according to Old Testament law. So even though Jesus Christ had commissioned His disciples to go preach the Gospel to all nations, not just to the Jewish peoples the Law was still influencing the Church of Jerusalem. The fear of breaking Old Testament beliefs about defilement had kept Peter and the rest of the disciples away from sharing the Gospel with even the Gentiles in their own nation of Israel. Now ten years down the road a Gentile man was seeking more truth about the character and nature of God. His name was Cornelius an Italian and a devout man who prayed often and gave alms to the people. Around 3pm, the afternoon hour of prayer Cornelius had a vision of Gods Angel coming to him directing to go get the apostle Peter at Joppa who would instruct Cornelius further about what to do about God.

As Peter was going up to housetop pray around noon Peter fell into this trance vision from the Holy Spirit. In the trance vision Peter saw heaven opened and a sheet descending spread out to all four corners, let down to the earth. Upon the sheet we're all manner of four-footed beasts, and wild beasts, and creeping things, and fowls of the air. Now according to Jewish Law these animals were forbidden by God for Jewish culture to eat. However, as Peter observed the vision of unclean animals, there came a voice from God which said rise Peter kill and eat. However, Peter had never violated Jewish dietary laws, and said not so Lord for I have never eaten anything which is common or unclean. Now the voice then spoke to Peter a second time and said, What God has cleansed, do not call common or unclean. This vision, and voice reaped two more times. After which was taken back up into heaven. Then the Gentiles arrived, and inquired wither Peter had resided there at the same time God had instructed Peter by the trance vision.

Now when Peter struggled to understand what the trance vision from God might mean, the Gentiles from Cornelius house arrived at the home where Peter just had the trance vision. The Gentiles inquired wither Peter had resided there, at the same time the Holy Spirit said three men are seeking you. Arise and go down and follow them doubting nothing for I have sent them. Here is the big issue, the Holy Spirit was directing Peter and the rest of the disciples unto a Gentile home where exposure to their lives would by Jewish Law make Peter and the other disciples unclean. However, by the Cross of Jesus Christ all mankind could be cleansed from their sins, both Jew and Gentiles.

Acts 10:11-20
11 And saw heaven opened, and a
certain vessel descending unto him, as it had been a great sheet knit at the four corners, and let down to the earth:
12 Wherein were all manner of four footed beasts of the earth, and wild beasts, and creeping
things, and fowls of the air.
13 And there came a

voice to him, Rise, Peter; kill, and eat.
14 But Peter said, Not so, Lord; for I
have never eaten any thing that is common or unclean.
15 And the voice spake unto him again the second
time, What God hath cleansed, that call not thou
common.
16 This was done thrice: and the vessel was received
up again into heaven.
17 Now while Peter doubted in himself what this
vision which he had seen should mean, behold, the
men which were sent from Cornelius had made
enquiry for Simon's house, and stood before the gate,
18 And called, and asked whether Simon, which was
surnamed Peter, were lodged there.
19 While Peter thought on the vision, the Spirit said
unto him, Behold, three men seek thee.
20 Arise therefore, and get thee
down, and go with them, doubting nothing: for I have
sent them.

Notice how Peter was being directed by the Lord
through a trance vision to fulfill what God had already
commissioned them to do ten years prior.
Acts 10:25-28
25 And as Peter was coming in, Cornelius met him, and
fell down at his feet, and worshipped him.
26 But Peter took him up, saying, Stand
up; I myself also am a man.
27 And as he talked with him, he went
in, and found many that were come together.

28 And he said unto them, Ye know how that it is an unlawful thing for a man that is a Jew to keep company, or come unto one of another nation; but God hath shewed me that I should not call man common or unclean.

Peter had to come understand the will of God to take the Gospel to the Gentile nations, making disciples of all nations. Being led of the Holy Spirit to confirm by revelation what God had already given prophetically in the Old Testament and was now being given to New Testament disciples by the means of visions.

Also notice how visions which come from God do not violate what God has given by the Scriptures. Why does this really matter? As visions from God are supernatural experiences which cannot be given upon demand from the will of man. Any person who teaches visions upon demand is not teaching the doctrines of the Bible. As within other religions, the New Age, and the occult are visions which come from other sources than from God the Holy Spirit. How dangerous are these days when lying dreams and visions are being promoted as the work of the Holy Spirit?

Marketing Dreams and Visions

Imagine living in a Church world where there is not internet, or any other form of an instant audience of hundreds or thousands of peoples. The only communication comes from your phone call, a few close friends, and Church family. Now God from time to time gives you prophetic dreams, and some are very alarming warning dreams. Since you only have a few people to share the dreams with, you bear the burden of the warning dreams in prayer. In no way are you able to create a sensational following, a platform of ministry, or any kind of popularity or financial gain. There is no push on your part to make a name for yourself, or have people identify you as a prophet. The Church is not pushing dreams and visions, so no sensationalism is present when a dream or vision comes from God. Have you ever considered this is how the Church of the first century Christians experienced the leading of the Holy Spirit?

What happens when marketing is taken out of the picture? No personal profit, no money, no fame, no glorification, or idolatry being pushed upon those who have dreams or a vision. The marketing of dreams and visions simply does not happen as there is no market for it. As the result, the Holy Spirit disperses the dreams and visions throughout the whole of the Church, and there are no exalted superstars, or self-proclaimed prophets. The central part of ministry comes from preaching and teaching the Written Word of God, and prayer, seeking knowledge and wisdom in these more foundational ways. The Church's mission is to make disciples so preaching the Gospel is always brought before the people as a main direction and focus. As making new disciples comes with a level of persecution and rejection the Church is not all caught up with mysticism and supernatural experiences. I trust this is the ordinary way God moves in His Church when the prophetic ministry is in proper order.

Now, how corrupting is the technique of marketing dreams and visions as prophetic words for the Churches consumption. The invasion of dreams and visions from all manner of peoples who are seeking an audience and want to profit from the Church. How Satan has gained a footing when the prophetic ministry can be bought and sold as a product. The purity and innocence are removed, and the restraints which prevent excess, and errors are lowered or eliminated altogether. Money, fame, prestige, and power are brought into play. It is no longer about dreams from God, visions from the Holy Spirit. Instead, it has become more about getting a word from God, so to have a platform. It is like the Church will market a man who always declaring I have a dream, God has given men a vision, or an angel came to visit me. It has become the sensation of Christians running after a man or woman who markets dreams and visions.

Let put this frankly, once you promote yourself you are doomed to marketing your ministry the rest of the time. In order to stay relevant, you must produce the next sensational dream, vision, or visitations. Your whole Christian experience will be reduced to producing revelations for Christians to consume for spiritual highs.

Today, this is the state of the modern Prophetic Movement is a big marketing machine spitting out thousands of prophetic words, predictions, dreams, visions, and angelic encounters. Those who are sucked in and trapped are forced to produce or lose their audience. Without a consumer driven audience there is no money to keep the self-proclaimed prophets in business. Those who stand outside and will not enter into the deception are constantly warning Christians of the Satanic traps.

How difficult for Christians who are seduced into following supernatural experiences and develop a craving for encounters which are spiritual in nature. A consuming culture has demanded the prophets must produce, or else lose any relevance which has made them rich and famous. Sadly, Satan has gained a large footprint, and is willing to supply the Prophetic Movement with all manner of lying, dreams, and visions. Only those who hunger for righteousness will escape the great lure of modern prophetic ministry.

Jeremiah 23:16-32
[16] Thus saith the LORD of hosts, hearken not unto the words of the prophets that prophesy unto you: they make you vain: they speak a vision of their own heart, and not out of the mouth of
the LORD.
[17] They say still unto them that despise me,
The LORD hath said, Ye shall have peace; and they say

unto everyone that walketh after the imagination of his own heart, no evil shall come upon you.

18 For who hath stood in the counsel of the LORD, and hath perceived and heard his word? who hath marked his word, and heard it?

19 Behold, a whirlwind of the LORD is gone forth in fury, even a grievous whirlwind: it shall fall grievously upon the head of the wicked.

20 The anger of the LORD shall not return, until he have executed, and till he have performed the thoughts of his heart: in the latter days ye shall consider it perfectly.

21 I have not sent these prophets, yet they ran: I have not spoken to them, yet they prophesied.

22 But if they had stood in my counsel, and had caused my people to hear my words, then they should have turned them from their evil way, and from the evil of their doings.

23 Am I a God at hand, saith the LORD, and not a God afar off?

24 Can any hide himself in secret places that I shall not see him? saith the LORD. Do not I fill heaven and earth? saith the LORD.

25 I have heard what the prophets said that prophesy lies in my name, saying, I have dreamed, I have dreamed.2

6 How long shall this be in the heart of the prophets that prophesy lies? yea, they are prophets of the deceit of their own heart;

27 Which think to cause my people to forget my name by their dreams which they tell every man to his

neighbour, as their fathers have forgotten my name for Baal.

28 The prophet that hath a dream, let him tell a dream; and he that hath my word, let him speak my word faithfully. What is the chaff to the wheat? saith the LORD.

29 Is not my word like as a fire? saith the LORD; and like a hammer that breaketh the rock in pieces?

30 Therefore, behold, I am against the prophets, saith the LORD, that steal my words everyone from his neighbour.

31 Behold, I am against the prophets, saith the LORD, that use their tongues, and say, He saith.

32 Behold, I am against them that prophesy false dreams, saith the LORD, and do tell them, and cause my people to err by their lies, and by their lightness; yet I sent them not, nor commanded them: therefore they shall not profit this people at all, saith the LORD.

What Is a Dream from God?

The major difference between a vision and a dream which God gives are both given by the Holy Spirit, but a vision happens during a time which the person is awake, while a dream is when the person is asleep. However, some visions happen when the person is asleep, and happens inside the persons dream, what is called a night vision.

Dreams from God are another form of Holy Spirit revelation which directs the person by using sleep and dreams to speak, give details, directions, and even future events. Even sometimes in dreams God angels can appear to give knowledge of Gods will. Of course, many dreams are not coming from God, and can come from other influences. Dreams can be a matter of one's own soul and events of the day, cares and worries which affect the subconscious mind influencing a person's dreams when asleep. Also, evil spirits can influence a persons sleep by invading their dreams with demonic thoughts and images. As the result Christians must be very discerning as to what their dreams are communicating. Is God the Holy Spirit speaking through a dream or series of dreams, and how should Christians judge its source and meanings.

Of course, dreams from God the Holy Sprit are from the Spirit of Prophecy, just like how the Holy Spirit can manifest through the gift of Prophecy. So, the written Word of God must measure all prophetic dreams to judge it according to Scriptural standards, like any other prophetic word.

How To Judge A Dream From God

"I love dreams. I love the contours of God's voice, the creativity He puts into His relationship with each of us. I enjoy interpreting dreams because every dream from God is an expression of His heart to the dreamer, and I get to see one more facet of His love.

In my last post, I addressed this question: "How do I know if my dream is from God?" I explained that dreams can come from one of three sources—the enemy, the human soul, or God—and I mentioned some of the ways we can recognize dreams from the enemy and dreams from the soul. In this post I want to explore how to recognize dreams from God.

Dreams, being a form of revelation, hold to the same rules as revelation. To be from God, a dream needs to do the following:

- Agree with Scripture;
- Carry the character of God and fit His personality;
- Be truthful, accurate;
- Bear good fruit;
- Point to Jesus; and
- Be full of color and light.

The Scripture Test

A dream from God will not violate what He has already revealed in Scripture. Like other forms of revelation, dreams are never intended to create doctrine or establish a rule of faith or practice for all people at all times—only the Bible can do such a thing.

It isn't a dream from God if it tells you to steal, commit adultery, murder, or violate any other moral commandment. Similarly, it isn't a dream from God if it tells you not to pray, that another god is God, that you shouldn't go to church or share your faith, that you shouldn't serve or give. Dreams from God will not change Scripture.

The Character Test
One of the keys to recognizing God's voice is knowing the difference between conviction and condemnation. Conviction is about activity, whereas condemnation is about identity. Conviction is specific, whereas condemnation is vague. Conviction cuts to the heart but leaves hope for change, while condemnation strips us of hope for change. When we are dealing with condemnation, we begin to believe the weight of our sin is so great that we will never be free.

The Holy Spirit shows us where we aren't living out the new life we have in Christ, so we can repent and come back to His heart. The enemy, meanwhile, slanders and accuses us until we are left hopeless and feeling defeated. When the Holy Spirit brings conviction, we can repent and turn back to His ways, and the weight of the conviction lifts. But when the enemy is condemning us, it doesn't matter how much we repent—it won't feel like enough.

A dream that leaves you feeling hopeless, like you will never be good enough for God or like you've done something that forever marks you and holds you back from His purpose for you—that is not a dream from God. It is from the enemy. Rebuke such dreams and don't believe them. Instead, ask God to show you His heart for you.

The Accuracy Test
The word *revelation* refers to something you didn't know previously. Just because a "revelation" is accurate doesn't mean it is from God (see Matthew 7:21–23). At the same time, God doesn't lie, so all revelation from Him will be accurate.

Understanding the difference between what is from God and what is not from God will keep us from chasing after deceptive signs, wonders, and even deceptive revelation. Though the accuracy test is important when determining if a dream is from God, the other tests need to be employed as well.

The Fruit Test
The fruit of the Spirit is love, joy, peace, patience, goodness, kindness, faithfulness, gentleness, and self-control (Galatians 5:22–23). A dream from God will never direct you to hate someone, become fearful, lose control, or accuse another person.

But if you have bitter jealousy and selfish ambition in your hearts, do not boast and be false to the truth. This is not the wisdom that comes down from above, but is

earthly, unspiritual, demonic. For where jealousy and selfish ambition exist, there will be disorder and every vile practice. But the wisdom from above is first pure, then peaceable, gentle, open to reason, full of mercy and good fruits, impartial and sincere.
— *James 3:14–17*

The Jesus Test
In Deuteronomy 13 and 18, God gives keys to recognizing true and false revelation. When discerning the source of a dream, this is the main question we should ask: "Does the revelation point us to a god other than Jesus?" The spirit of prophecy is the testimony of Jesus (Revelation 19:10), which means that all true revelation will lead us to Him.

Did the dream tempt you to put your trust in anything other than Jesus? Or did it cause your heart to fall more in love with Him?

The Color Test
God is light, and around His throne is a rainbow of color. The Bible often
uses *light* versus *dark* and *day* versus *night* as metaphors for good and evil, God and Satan. A dream from God will often be full of color and bright light.

The Main Thing to Remember
The foundation of discerning your dreams is relationship. As you draw closer to God, He will reveal

what is from Him and what is not. If you approach dreams and supernatural experiences from a position of relationship, you will find yourself walking on safe, steady ground. Your Father is good, and He wants to speak to you. When you ask Him for bread, He won't give you a stone (Luke 11:11–13)."
Dream Foundation pt. 3 John Thomas
Streamsministiresinternational.com

Holding Fast the Head

What happens when the Church loses grip of the head of the Church Jesus Christ? Worship becomes about someone or something else. What has happened to the preaching and worship of Jesus Christ as the central reason for the Church. You might go to Church today and not even hear the name of Jesus Christ mentioned even one time. The preaching could be about politics, or saving the 7 Mountains of culture, or bringing heaven to earth, or speaking with angels, or traveling by spirit into heaven to hold court against Satan. All these are the modern philosophical beliefs which drives large portions of the modern Church. While the other half of the Church is invested into social causes, like feeding and clothing the poor, or providing safe drinking water, or medical care. Of course, all these are important causes and should not be neglected. However, what is neglected is the preaching of eternal salvation and the reaching of the lost with the message of the Cross of Jesus Christ. Saving a person from their impoverished environment is one thing, while saving a man from eternal damnation is of greater significance.

When did it not become about Jesus Christ anymore? I know in the Charismatic Movement a great shift came when it was no longer good enough for Jesus Christ to save the world and transitioned to the Church saving the world. Simply put, many Charismatics have a greater emphasis in modern day apostles than they do with Jesus Christ. Of course, none dare admit this is the true condition of the Movement today, but unless you promise spiritual event in Charismatic conferences you will not draw a large audience. Has anyone noticed it became about predicting the next big event, or the next great move of God? Massive amounts of time and effort, and expense spent on "how God would save the world through a big Church revival." The Charismatics have lost confidence in the preaching of the Cross, and it has become about the Great Apostolic/ Prophetic move of God.

It was no longer about the souls of men and preaching about the blood of Jesus Christ for eternal redemption. Instead, the Gospel became about the Kingdom and saving culture and nations. Many of the head apostles of the Movement now preach there are two Gospels. One which saves men's souls called the Gospel of Salvation, and the other called the Gospel of the Kingdom which saves nations. Of course, this is a complete perversion as the Gospel of Salvation saves both souls and nations. Just not the way modern day apostles teach.

Of course, as no nations or cities have been transformed into a Christian government on earth, new philosophies were added to the false Gospel. Now we have a constant diet of going into heaven upon demand. After going into heaven, the next big thing was talking with angels. Once in heaven it is about talking with Gods angels and speaking with dead prophets like Elijah. Of course, this is all accomplished through heavenly encounters and for the right price a modern-day apostle will teach you how to contact and communicate with your own personal angel.

Let us not forget the subjective nature of these visions or heavenly encounters. It is not like visions we see in the Scriptures of Heaven. Instead, those modern days prophets who go into heaven and see a version of heaven which no one else has encountered, not even the original apostles of Jesus Christ.

However, alarming this is to those outside the Apostolic Movement, it has led many in the Charismatics to believe modern day apostles are even more advanced than the apostle Paul. Modern apostles are thought to bring new light of understanding into worn out interpretations of the Bible. Of course, advanced understanding by these Charismatic leaders does not have anything to do with a deeper richer insight into the Cross of Jesus Christ. Instead, it is about how man is becoming more like God, or how the Church is filling up with Gods divinity so Jesus Christ will first return through the Church. After the Church has saved the world.

As all this false doctrine and practice has not brought revival or made for even one Christian city or nation. A super spirituality has also been adopted to dangle the carrot which drives the false doctrines and beliefs. As the result the next big experience is angels, spirit travel, dreams and visions, getting a spiritual high, or the next big revival. It is never about the person of Jesus Christ. At what cost though? The greatest departure from Bible morality and Bible foundations has happened at the same time. One third of Evangelicals does not believe Jesus Christ is God.

The cost is man playing God, and the Church emptying from the person of Jesus Christ. Instead, you have all your angels of light filling the Church with New Age spirits. Or you can repent and get back to authentic Christian faith. As Jesus Christ will have no other gods before Him. Even if it is the most celebrated names of men in Charismatic acclaim. These men are not God, or even a divine being, or even filling up with the divinity of God. At best they are clay jars full of themselves.

The Failure of Angel Worship

In the Charismatic Movement the height of spirituality has become heavenly encounters. Has this emphasis about going into heaven and speaking with angels, or dead prophets what Christianity teaches? The answer is defiantly no. It is a counterfeit Gospel and here is why. The Scriptures teach Jesus Christ is superior to angels, and the prophets. Here is the simple reason, Jesus Christ is God creator of angels and the prophets. Greater is the one who made all things than those who are created.

Let us say you go into heaven (mostly fake or demonic), and you say you meet an angel, or a dead prophet from the Old Testament like Elijah. You speak of the greatness of the spiritual encounter of all the wisdom and secret knowledge you gained from angels, or dead prophets. What is wrong with this picture? Heaven is Gods Throne, all of Heaven is acclimated towards the Throne of God in adoration and worship. Why, because all wisdom and knowledge come from the Throne and God who gives it. The Supremacy of Jesus Christ is emphasized in heaven, and on earth, and throughout all creation. The most glorious of heavenly beings bow down throwing their crowns at the feet of Jesus Christ on the Throne. If you went to heaven your conversation would be all about the Supremacy of Jesus Christ.

Now let us look at angel worship deception. Of course, all the heavenly travelers of the Charismatic Movement will say they do not worship angels or heavenly encounters. A poor excuse for all the time, conferences, and money which is poured into the Charismatic Movement on how to go into heaven upon demand. Why all the emphasis about heaven being a Jell-O room for Kids (One of the prophet's explanations while being in heaven), and various versions of sitting on the lap of God? When the Bible says God lives in unapproachable light which no man can enter or has seen Gods face. What is wrong with all these visions and heavenly encounters. It has the hollow ring of a Jesus Christ which is more like a man than God. Also, a heaven which has more excitement about the "things of heaven," than God in Supremacy upon the Throne as shown in the Book of Revelation.

1 Timothy 6:12-16
 12 Fight the good fight of faith, lay hold
on eternal life, whereunto thou art also called, and hast
professed a good profession before many witnesses.
13 I give thee charge in the sight of God, who quickeneth all
things, and before Christ Jesus, whobefore Pontius Pilat
e witnessed a good confession;
14 That thou keep this commandment without
spot, unrebukeable, until the appearing of
our LordJesus Christ:
15 Which in his times he shall shew, who is the
blessed and only Potentate, the King of
kings, andLord of lords;
16 Who only hath immortality, dwelling in the

light which no man can approach unto; whom no man hath seen, nor can see: to
whom be honour and power everlasting. Amen.

Angel worship is a complete failure and a gross danger because it does not demonstrate the supremacy of Jesus Christ. The Gospel message is Jesus Christ and the Cross for the salvation of the world. Angels and prophets do not have esoteric wisdom and knowledge which can only be gained by going into heaven. The Charismatics who are profiting off angels, and their secret mysteries are con men and false prophets. It is a platform of sensuous minds who refuse to hold fast the head Jesus Christ. False prophets can travel by demonic sensations into a world of angels of light who are imitating as Gods angels, or even God Himself. The greatest heresy of our day comes from all those who emphasize Heaven, or heaven to earth. Heaven and earth encounters, angels and dead prophets are all grossly inferior to Jesus Christ and the Cross of Jesus Christ.

Do not let any so-called prophet, or apostle lead you into angel worship by sensuous visions of inflated self-glorification. Jesus Christ is the glory of the Church as there is no man, no angel, in heaven, on earth, or under the earth to whom every knee will not bow and their tongues confess Jesus Christ is the Lord of Glory. This is Jesus Christ in whom God the Father has declared the Son, having given a more excellent inheritance and better name than angels. God commanded all the angels to worship the Son in His supremacy obtained by the Incarnation and conquest of the Cross. The angels bow down to the Incarnated glorified Son of God whose Throne was obtained by conquest of the Cross and Resurrection. All who fail to preach Jesus Christ in absolute supremacy are just the modern-day magicians pretending to be the prophets of God.

Colossians 2:18-19
18 Let no man beguile you of your reward in a voluntary humility and worshipping of angels, intruding into those things which he hath not seen, vainly puffed up by his fleshly mind,
19 And not holding the Head, from which all the body by joints and bands having nourishment ministered, and knit together, increaseth with the increase of God.

Hebrews 1
1 God, who at sundry times and in divers manners spake in time past unto the fathers by the prophets,
2 Hath in these last days spoken unto us by his Son, whom he hath appointed heir of all things, by whom also he made the worlds;
3 Who being the brightness of his glory, and the express image of his person, and upholding all things by the word of his power, when he had by himself purged our sins, sat down on the right

hand of the Majesty on high;

4 Being made so much better than the angels, as he hath by inheritance obtained a more excellent name than they.

5 For unto which of the angels said he at any time, Thou art my Son, this day have I begotten thee? And again, I will be to him a Father, and he shall be to me a Son?

6 And again, when he bringeth in the first begotten into the world, he saith, And let all the angels of God worship him.

7 And of the angels he saith, Who maketh his angels spirits, and his ministers a flame of fire.

8 But unto the Son he saith, Thy throne, O God, is for ever and ever: a sceptre of righteousness is the sceptre of thy kingdom.

9 Thou hast loved righteousness, and hated iniquity; therefore God, even thy God, hath anointed thee with the oil of gladness above thy fellows.

10 And, Thou, Lord, in the beginning hast laid the foundation of the earth; and the heavens are the works of thine hands:

11 They shall perish; but thou remainest; and they all shall wax old as doth a garment;

12 And as a vesture shalt thou fold them up, and they shall be changed: but thou art the same, and thy years shall not fail.

13 But to which of the angels said he at any

time, Sit on my right hand, until . thine enemies thy
footstool?
14 Are they not all ministering spirits, sent
forth to minister for them who shall be heirs of
salvation?

Chapter Fourteen
Visions of Jesus Christ

Does Jesus Christ ever appear in visions for a Christian?
The answer is found in the Book of Revelation when
Jesus Christ appears to the apostle John. The initial
vision has been documented in chapter one of the Book
of Revelation.

Revelation 1:10-11
10 I was in the
Spirit on the Lord's day, and heard behind me a great vo
ice, as of a trumpet,
11 Saying, I am Alpha and Omega, the first and the
last: and, What thou seest, write in a book, and
send it unto the seven churches which
are in Asia; unto Ephesus, and unto Smyrna, and untoPe
rgamos, and unto Thyatira, and unto Sardis, and unto Ph
iladelphia, and unto Laodicea.
10 I was in the
Spirit on the Lord's day, and heard behind me a great vo
ice, as of a trumpet,
11 Saying, I am Alpha and Omega, the first and the
last: and, What thou seest, write in a book, and

send it unto the seven churches which
are in Asia; unto Ephesus, and unto Smyrna, and untoPe
rgamos, and unto Thyatira, and unto Sardis, and unto Ph
iladelphia, and unto Laodicea.

The vision of Jesus Christ first started with the voice of
the Lord instructing the apostle John to write down the
things which he was about to see and hear. In writing
down the visions given
The vision of Jesus Christ first started with the voice of
the Lord instructing the apostle John to write down the
things which he was about to see and hear. In writing
down the visions given
John in the island of Patmos we now have the record
given in the book of Revelation. Once again Jesus Christ
gave the interpretations of the symbols, and John was
not allowed to inject his own private revelations with
these visions.

When John turned to see who was speaking, John first
saw seven golden candle sticks, and standing in the
middle of the candle sticks was one like the Son of Man,
Jesus Christ. Jesus Christ was dressed as the High Priest
of Heaven which matches other passages of Scriptures
like written in the book of Hebrews. Jesus Christ our
Great High Priest of the Heavenly Temple. Jesus Christ
was clothed with a priestly garment down to the foot,
and around his breast was a golden girdle which would
match what the High Priest of the Old Testament.

The appearance of Jesus Christ as God is also revealed in John's vision. John saw Jesus Christ as the glorified Lord God of Heaven who appearance was so glorious John fell as a dead man before the vision of Jesus Christ. The head of Jesus Christ was as the ancient of days, His head and hairs were white like wool, as white as snow, and the eyes of Jesus Christ burned the eternal Spirit of God. The feet of Jesus Christ burned like fine brass, which was superheated in a furnace, speaking of Gods power to judge both the heavens and the earth. As Jesus spoke the sound of a mighty roaring voice of many waters came forth.

Out of the mouth of the Lord went a sharp two-edged sword which the Scriptures teach is the living Word of God. By which the Lord judges all His creation, as nothing can be hidden for the sight of God. All things are open and naked to been seen unto Him to who we must give an account. The face of Jesus Christ shone as the strength of the sun which speaks of His ultimate glory.

12 And I turned to see the
voice that spake with me. And being turned, I
saw seven golden candlesticks;
13 And in the midst of
the seven candlesticks one like unto the Son of
man, clothed with a garment down to the
foot, and girt about the paps with a golden girdle.
14 His head and his hairs were white like wool, as white

as snow; and his eyes were as a flame of fire;
15 And his feet like unto fine brass, as if they
burned in a furnace; and his voice as the sound of many
waters.

Now when visions are given by the Holy Spirit, the
Scriptures themselves are instrumental in giving the
symbols their true meanings. In this case Jesus Christ
Himself tells the apostle John what each of the symbols
John saw really meant.

16 And he had in his right
hand seven stars: and out of his mouth went a sharp tw
oedged sword: andhis countenance was as the
sun shineth in his strength.

One must ask when men have seen the Lord of Glory
the fall like dead men? Even when the Lord's angels
have appeared in a vision, great fear and dread
accompanies the Angel of the Lord. In authentic visions
the magnificence of Gods glory and exaltation are
always present, even when it is just angels sent by God
as messengers to the saints.

17 And when I saw him, I fell at his feet as dead. And he
laid his right hand upon me, saying unto
me, Fear not; I am the first and the last:

When John falls as a dead man, Jesus Christ declares His
triumph over death, Hell, and the grave. Jesus Christ is

declaring what John had already seen and know while Jesus Christ was still on the earth for forty days after His resurrection from the dead.

18 I am he that liveth, and was dead; and, behold, I am alive for evermore, Amen; and have keys of and of death.

Notice visions from God are always redemptive in purpose. They are not given to exalt the man, as visions are the testimony of Jesus Christ the Spirit of Prophecy which always exalt the Lord. In John's vision of Jesus Christ, he is given instructions on how to record the events of the Church age now, and what would follow by the coming Tribulation and the end of the age. Notice how the written Word of God and visions of Jesus Christ are in complete agreement. No man who professes he had a vision of Jesus Christ, then says Jesus taught him to add or subtract from what has already been written in the Scriptures has been given a true vision.

19 Write the things which thou hast seen, and the things which are, and the things which shall be hereafter;
20 The mystery of the seven stars which thou sawest in my right hand, and the seven golden candlesticks. The seven stars are the angels of the seven churches: and the seven candlesticks which thou sawest are the seven churches.

Here Is an Example of a False Vision of Jesus

Bible of the Charismatic 7 Mountain Movement is called the Passion Translation Bible.
"In his interview, Simmons claims that Jesus personally took him to a library room in heaven, and that Jesus promised to bring him back to heaven and give him a brand new chapter of the gospel of John that has never yet been known—John chapter 22. Here is the TV interview of the author of the Passion Translation Bible.

Sid Roth: (SR) "my guest found himself in the library of heaven (ooh), and he saw books on ever subject you can imagine, books on science, and medicine, things like cancer cures that have not even occurred yet and then he saw one book that was called John 22. There are only 21 books in the gospel of John, twenty-two had to do with the next great, greatest revival the world has ever seen..."

 Big difference. Okay. How in the world did you get into the library room of Heaven? I want to go there."

Brian Simmons (BS): Well, you know, as believers in Christ, there's only one entrance into the realm of the spirit, and that is the name of Yeshua, the name of Jesus Christ. We don't work it up. We don't get into an ecstatic state on our own. I was actually asleep, and I was taken out of my body, and I was brought into this immense library room. I loved being there. And the Lord came up to me and he said, "Brian, I have brought you here to let you take any two books you want." And I'm just walking around. But it didn't take long before I saw a book that I knew I was to have and then soon I saw another book I knew I was to have. But you'll never want me back on the show when I tell you what happened then."

SR: What?

BS: "Well I have to tell you the truth. I saw a third book and I knew the Lord told me I could only take two. And in Heaven, whatever you think is put out over the loudspeaker, everyone hears it. Your thoughts are broadcasted. So, here's what I hear coming out of the loudspeaker, and it's my own thoughts, how can I steal this book. And then I said, oh, no, I'm shoplifting on God. I felt so ashamed. But I knew if I could take this book, there was this book, so, if I could just take this book back with me to the natural realm it would trigger awakening in all the nations of the earth. It would bring, it would make the name of Jesus famous in the world. But Jesus came to me and said, "Brian, I cannot let you take this book." And he looked at me in the eyes with love that melted me, and he said, "You are not ready for that book." Then he promised that, "I will bring you back one day and I will give you that book."

SR: What was the title?
BS: Written on the cover of the book was John 22.

SR: But there's only 21 chapters in John. What's this 22?

BS: Well John 22, go back to John 14:12 and you'll see that there is a greater works generation. "The works that I do you will do even greater works than these." I believe the John 22 generation will be a people that do the greater works of Jesus. They will not add to the scripture, and that's a sealed book. But it is a book that is unfolding, and the works of Jesus will be replicated by an entire generation of people that believe fully in the power of God."

https://sidroth.org/television/tv-archives/brian-simmons

When Will the Charismatic Movement Address the Delusion of Brian Simmons

The author of the Passion Translation has changed the meanings of hundreds if not thousands of Scriptures by adding or subtracting words to the original passages. As no Apostle or Prophet of the modern-day Apostolic Reformation protested, Simmons has been given free rein to go even further to bring his delusional statements about what the Bible says even further. Simmons has completely dismantled the Book of Revelation into meanings which never before have ever been interpreted in Simmons way. If Simmons can change the meanings of Scriptures calling it hidden treasure never before understood, then Simmons alone is the only person in history who has been given the ability to accurately interpret the Scriptures. If this be the case the whole Church must turn to Simmons and make corrections from Scriptural beliefs which have been held for almost 2000 years. Or Simmons has gone off the rails?

Look at the insanity Brian Simmons is attempting to teach conceding who the body of Christ is. In Simmons own words a "reincarnation of Jesus Christ." Is this a slip of the tongue, or the decisions of a false apostles who has fallen to evil spirit and writes doctrines of demons?

Here Is Simmons own words:
"The sealed book is you. He's the Word, the volume of the book it is written of Him. We express the Word. WE ARE THE WORD MADE FLESH AGAIN. WE ARE THE REINCARNATION OF JESUS CHRIST. The corporate expression."

Brian Simmons is teaching the 7 Sealed Book of Revelation 5 is about Christians being reincarnated into Jesus Christ. Is this ever been what the historical Church from its inception unto today has ever taught? The Church is becoming Christ in the flesh?

Christ is no longer a man, instead the Church is becoming Jesus Christ in the flesh. Do you realize

Simmons is putting men who are born again into the same nature and person as the only begotten Son of God. Simmons is making gods out of Christians, as the Church is becoming Christ in the flesh. This is a blasphemous statement and should shock Charismatics who have endorsed this insanity.

Simmons quote of Christians becoming Christ, who is no longer a person!

"We're the seed of Christ, the 42nd generation, we complete the genealogy of Jesus. CHRIST IS NO LONGER A MAN, HE'S A PEOPLE. YOU AND I CARRY LIKE MARY. WE WILL BRING FORTH THE CHRIST. THE SECOND COMING IS THE BECOMING OF THE LORD. The Father loves the Son so much, he is going to fill the earth with people just like Him."

So instead of the actual person of Jesus Christ returning to the earth, Simmons has Jesus Christ returning in the corporate man, the Church. Simmons teaches the heretical position of Preterist who need no bodily return of Jesus Christ, as that is fulfilled in the Corporate Man Jesus the Church.

"The earth will be my footstool. There will be a feet company that will represent me on earth. When a mother gives birth, what's the last part of the body to come forth. Feet. The feet. There will be a feet company. AS THE CHRIST COMES FORTH AND EMERGES

ON THE EARTH IN A CORPORATE EXPRESSION, there will be a people who will become the feet. The beautiful feet. How beautiful are the feet. God will, uh, you know, God will soon crush Satan under YOUR FEET."

Simmons like other New Apostolic Reformation apostles before him like Bill Hammond teach Christians will overcome sin, and death as they become the corporate man Jesus on the earth.

"There will be a feet company, a Satan crushing company that will devour, like a threshing sledge, they will devour every work of the enemy. THEY WILL BE UNTOUCHED BY SIN, DARKNESS, EVEN DEATH."

Simmons in typical fashion of New Apostolic Reformation declares new light on old interpretations of Scriptures there by changing the foundations of Christianity into Brian Simmons sect.

In Brian Simmons words the Antichrist are all those beliefs which are now outdated and irrelevant. The book of Revelation according to Simmons has no person as the Antichrist just the old-fashioned beliefs of Gods judgment which has blocked the Charismatics from making the world the Garden of Eden once again:

"Don't look now, but I found the antichrist. Deal with it. Get him out. Stop being in love with your tradition, opinion and understanding of the Bible that's so shallow, and so, like, feeble, and we barely make it in our lives because we don't have that rich treasure yet. We've not unlocked the deepest places of spirit life [indecipherable]. Where we bring healing because of a touch or a word that speaks and life comes forth."

"The natural elements, the natural realm, will be destroyed. And we will become the paradise of God once again. When God said, I have made you in my image and my likeness, now rule and take dominion. To the measure we carry his image and likeness, to that measure we rule and take dominion. You can't rule and take dominion without the image and likeness. You guys getting this? We know a little about image."

Who within the New Apostolic Reformation will break with the ranks, and before has protected Brian Simmons by covering up for him? It's time to see this hypocrisy throughout the whole of the NAR come to light before another Joseph Smith arises to lead hundreds of millions into deep demonic deception.

Conclusion
Jesus Christ Our Example

Perhaps you have often heard Jesus Christ is our example which Christians should imitate or follow. Usually, the exhortations center around some measure of how Christians should display power and conquest. Millions of hours in sermons are devoted to say how

Jesus Christ did miracles as a man, so what ever Jesus Christ could do, Christians so do also. The Scriptures most often quoted is then John fourteen, truly, truly. I say unto you the works I do; you will do and even greater works than these." The emphasis is on conquering and rule, and being kings, or apostles who walk in great dominion and power.

However, how would an original apostle describe the example of Jesus Christ which Christians are most closely to imitate. Great power, Kingship, dominion, rule, spreading the kingdom all over the earth, or even taking Satan to court in heaven? If there was ever a man who knew how to model the power of God, it was the apostle, Peter. The Book of Acts records how the shadow of Peter could produce miracles so even the crippled would be restored as Peter passed by. This apostle of power, signs, and wonders left us a record, a testimony on how Christians should follow after the example of the Lord.

1 Peter 2:21
21 For even hereunto were ye called: because Christ also suffered for us, leaving us an example, that ye should follow his steps.

Did you get that? The example Peter taught Christians to follow Jesus Christ in modeling, "the example of suffering," that Christians should follow in His footsteps. The example apostle Peter teaches is the Cross, Jesus

Christ who suffered with injustice, victimization, rejection, abuse, and did not deny the Cross. What is the problem with modern apostles? The absence of preaching the Cross, and the evidence of suffering by engaging non-Christian peoples.

Have you noticed everything is done in theory by modern apostles? Practical suffering is not present in America men who identify as apostles. They speak of taking over the world, of the Christianizing the nations, and conquering the earth by power. However, their world is from mega Churches to mega Church conferences where they collect millions of dollars. Live in lavish homes and drive exotic cars. They have become multimillions and live off Christians and their reputations of greatness.

Peter knew the cost of preaching the Cross to hostile peoples, being whipped, and beaten, even when Peter demonstrated God's miraculous power. Peter knew it was not miracles which would convict the world instead it was the Cross. Instead picking up the Cross and walking in the example of suffering for the Lord. Modern day apostles are known for their boasts of worldly wealth and success, while the original apostles all died as "martyrs for Jesus Christ."

Finally, what is the power of the Holy Spirit for? To show the world how great Christians are? How powerful, how kingly, how conquering? Jesus Christ said to His apostles you shall receive power to be my "martos," that's martyr in the Greek (Acts 1:8) Did you get that, Jesus Christ expected His apostles would suffer in the like manner through accepting the Cross. The power of the Holy Spirit is to give the saints the capacity to follow the example of Jesus Christ is suffering to be His witness. No wonder the Church is stuck behind the four walls and talking about conquering the world by "charismatic kingdom power."

To get out from behind the lust for power and wealth and engage non-Christians will bring the "real example of Jesus Christ," back into the Church.

1 Peter 2:22-25
22 Who did no sin, neither was guile found in his mouth:
23 Who, when he was reviled, reviled not again; when he suffered, he threatened not; but committed himself to him that judgeth righteously:
24 Who his own self bare our sins in his own body on the tree, that we, being dead to sins, should live unto righteousness: by whose stripes ye were healed.
 25 For ye were as sheep going astray; but are now returned unto the Shepherd and Bishop of your souls.

The Holy Spirit Upon Demand

Can a Christian call for the Holy Spirit upon demand? So many signs and wonders Charismatics are looking for supernatural phenomena which they attribute to the

Holy Spirit. In the extreme prophetic visions upon demand, or heavenly encounters upon demand are being taught from many platforms. So, can a Christian simply by self-will, and personal desire will themselves into a supernatural vision, or heavenly visit? Can a Christian go into heaven, encounter angels, or have visions or visitations upon demand? The answer lies in the fact wither or not Christians can direct the Holy Spirit. Is the Christian faith given Christians the ability to direct and manage the Holy Spirit?

Since all these experiences are recorded in the Bible and are genuine experiences given by God, Christians can experience them. Even when the Holy Spirit was poured out on the day of Pentecost, Peter speaks of young men having visions, and old men having dreams. So, with the Person of the Holy Spirit comes prophetic experiences like dreams and visions.

Acts 2:17
"And it shall come to pass in the last days, saith God, I will   pour out of my Spirit upon all flesh: and your sonsand your da ughters shall   prophesy, and your young   men shall see visions, and your old men shall dream dreams.."

So, the fact supernatural acts do happen from the presence of the Holy Spirit is a Scriptural fact. However, can Christian's control and direct those experiences upon demand? The answer is absolutely not, a Spirit filled

Christian is to be led of the Holy Spirit yielding their will to God's will.

Romans 8:14
"For as many as are led by the Spirit of God, they are the sons of God."

What a vast difference for Christians to be led of the Holy Spirit, as compared to direct the Holy Spirit according to man's will. In truth it is "impossible to direct God the Holy Spirit." So why all the emphasis teaching about spiritual experiences upon demand? This can lead to only a few conclusions: 1) God isn't responding to man's manipulation 2) The supernatural phenomena are not the result of the Holy Spirit 3) Demonic Spirits are involved and are imitating the presence of God 4) Human abilities are involved including physic or occult phenomena.

So, with the impossibility of men directing the Holy Spirit an artificial event is manifesting which some signs and wonders Christians have come to believe is the Holy Spirit. The push to create supernatural events upon demand has opened the door for deception. A belief God will honor the desires of Christians to satiate their thirst for supernatural occurrences has introduced foreign elements into the Christian faith. Just because Christians want to experience supernatural power and are sincere in their pursuit does not guarantee they cannot be deceived by demonic imitations. Sincerity is not a guard to stop evil spirits attempting to deceive unsuspecting Christians. For signs and wonders teachers to suggest God will protect sincere Christians when seeking for supernatural signs and wonders is an absolute misconception. The devil loves to play off ignorance in order to conceal his activities, so evil spirits will often attempt to mimic the presence of God.

God will not respond to every demand Christians attempt in their pursuit of the supernatural. Miracles are not an end unto themselves, as God will not do signs and wonders simply to demonstrate His power. The miracles, signs and wonders worked by the Holy Spirit always demonstrate the authenticity of Jesus Christ. The working of the Holy Spirit is always to point to Jesus Christ, and to confirm the message of the Cross. Many signs and wonders Charismatics have been caught up into sensational supernatural phenomena which do not conclude in Jesus Christ. Instead point to a man, or end in themselves. Signs and wonders which glorify a man, or a ministry creates many temptations and problems for people to take their eyes off the Lord and put them upon a man. Scriptures reveal when the Holy Spirit worked a mighty miracle through one of the original apostles, or the apostle Paul, extra care would be taken to give all the glory to Jesus Christ. When a miracle, or someone who God has used takes the miracle unto themselves; you can be sure the Holy Spirit has been grieved, or evil spirits are involved.

When miracles, signs, and wonders are pursued for their own sake deception is sure to follow. Christians are never exhorted to seek supernatural phenomena, never does the Scriptures teach Christians to seek visions upon demand, and trips into the spirit world, or communication with angels, or power to show signs and wonders. Instead, all Christians are to be led of the Holy Spirit, receive power of the Holy Spirit to be a witness (Martyr) and to pick up the Cross in self denial to follow Jesus Christ as His witness. In the context of preaching the Gospel these signs will follow those who believe:

Mark 16:15-18
"And he said unto them, Go ye into all the world, and preach the gospel to every creature. He that believeth and is baptized shall be saved; but he that believeth not shall be damned. And these signs shall follow them that believe; In my name shall they cast out devils; they shall speak with new tongues; They shall take up serpents; and if they drink any deadly thing, it shall not hurt them; they shall lay hands on the sick, and they shall recover."

Notice how signs follow the preaching of the gospel, as a confirmation to the message of the Cross. Signs which follow the Gospel message have a very direct purpose in glorifying Jesus Christ and drawing attention to the truth of the Cross. Notice how the signs connected to the preaching of the Gospel mainly have to do with a "demonstration of salvation;" resulting in casting out of evil spirits, or physical healing of diseases. The other two signs speak of supernatural protection to God's messengers, or the presence of the gifts of the Holy Spirit. (Tongues) All these supernatural signs have their basis in Scriptures, and were in the teachings and ministry of Jesus Christ, and demonstrated by the original apostles. The whole Church has been given to pray for the sick and demonized to confirm the authority Christians have been given in Jesus Christ name. Notice how signs related related to the preaching of the gospel are "very specific," and have their basis completely in works of salvation. The signs and wonders demonstrated by the Holy Spirit bring glory to Jesus Christ resulting in works of salvation, healing, deliverance which result in freeing humanity from sin and demonic bondage.

The Holy Spirit is committed to Biblical signs and wonders which result in the glorification of Jesus Christ, and which demonstrated the power of salvation. These signs are down according to the will of God, and according to Christians meeting certain conditions like the preaching of the Gospel. In this way the will of God is know concerning how signs and wonders work, so as not to be confused with demonic counterfeits. Also, the Holy Spirit will not be controlled by the desires of any man for the supernatural which have no purpose in the work of God. As the result Christians can test the authenticity of miracles, and their origin. The Bible commands the saints to test the Spirit, as many deceivers operate inside the house of God, the Church.

Here are some simple ways Jesus Christ taught His disciples to discern the work of the Holy Spirit: (John 14: 6-7 & 26; 15:26; 16:7-9 &13)

1) The Holy Spirit is sent to lead and guide Christians; the Holy Spirit will abide with faithful Christians the rest of their lives.
2) The Holy Spirit is given after Jesus Christ ascended into heaven; He is the Comforter who comes to assist believers in their walk of faith.
3) The Holy Spirit is the Spirit of Truth and cannot participate in deception
4) God the Holy Spirit was sent by God the Father, as the Comforter who comes in place of Jesus Christ after the ascension.
5) The Holy Spirit teaches what Jesus Christ has already said and brings them to the saint's remembrance. The Holy Spirit will not violate what has already been written in the Word of God.
6) The Holy Spirit will only testify of Jesus Christ and bring Him glory only. Also, the Holy Spirit will only be sent from God the Father, only according to His will.
7) The Holy Spirit is the Spirit of truth and will not compromise the Word of God. The Holy Spirit's Character is Holy resulting in exposure of lies, and the conviction of sin.
8) Conviction is one of the major attributes of the presence of the Holy Spirit, He will reprove the world of sin, and God's righteousness, and of God's judgment.

9) Holy Spirit confronts mankind's need for Jesus Christ.
10)The Holy Spirit is to lead and guide Christians into all truth. Christians do not lead the Holy Spirit instead must be led.
11) The Holy Spirit will not speak of Himself, but what he hears. All inspiration is from God, not man. The Holy Spirit will never speak a false prophecy or give a false prophetic future prediction.

With all the Biblical guidelines in place the Church can discern if the signs originate from the Holy Spirit or some other source. In the Charismatic signs and wonders movement many of these restraints have been violated, allowing for foreign elements to be introduced into the Christian faith. If signs and wonders Charismatic Christians don't follow the Holy Spirit into His will and way, instead violate the will of God pushing for supernatural power where do the phenomena come? As mentioned earlier there are two other possible sources of the supernatural one from evil spirits and the other from physic phenomena, or occult.

Experiences In the Holy Spirit

For most of the time Christians are walking by faith
being led of the Holy Spirit apart from any experiences.
This is the normal Christin faith, not supernatural
experiences upon demand. What should the real
constant Christian experience really be like? For those
Christians who are willing to share their faith in nations

and governments which are hostile to Christianity, it is persecution, injustice, suffering, and even martyrdom. The true constant is to pick up the Cross in self-denial without any spiritual highs, or immediate gratifications. Just the knowledge of complete obedience to Jesus Christ, a willingness to suffer loss in this age trusting the Lord to recommence your life at His Second Coming.

When Christianity loses it salt, it has eliminated the Cross the offense of confronting men in the sin and spiritual darkness. Jesus Christ taught men love the darkness rather than the light because their deeds are evil. Men who love the darkness won't come to the light to have their evil deeds exposed. The one true constant is the preaching of the Cross and for Christians is the power of God, while for mankind lost in darkness it is pure foolishness. So, do modern Christians expect spiritually dead men to sympathize with the Church to accept the confrontation of their sin? Warning them to escape the wrath to come, the condemnation of Hell fire?

The Holy Spirits true character in work is 3 main things:
1) The Holy Spirit will reprove the world of sin.
2) The Holy Spirit will reprove the world of righteousness.
3) The Holy Spirit will reprove the world of judgment.

Of sin because they believe not in Jesus Christ as the Lord God, and Savior of the World.

Of righteousness, because of Christ's Resurrection in power over sin and death, the perfect sacrifice, now seated at the right hand of the Father. Of judgement because the Prince of the World, Satan has been judged in the Cross, and will be placed in the Lake of Fire after the final judgment. All men who follow the Antichrist, who worship Satan, will also inherit the judgement of Satan being cast into the Lake of Fire with him.

Now the work of the Holy Spirit brings Christians in conflict with the world, and at war with Satan, and the Kingdom of Darkness. This is the "true experience" of Christians who truly walk with the Lord. The true works of the Holy Spirit have not changed with the modern Church.

So, what has been the problem? The substitution of authentic works of the Holy Spirit, for spiritual counterfeits, which have no personal loss or cross. Have you noticed how little modern-day apostles, or signs and wonders Christians speak of suffering for the Lord. Of course, modern apostles live from Christian conference to conference, where their "egos are stoked," and they make millions of dollars selling a Cross less gospel. The true apostle has his testimony in experiencing the loss of all things to witness the testimony of Jesus Christ. Notice how Jesus Christ taught His apostles they would receive power to be a martyr, (witness), when they were filled with the Holy Spirit. Ironically, all the original apostles were put to death for their faith as martyrs, only the apostle John made it to old age. How many modern-day apostles would be willing to die for the faith, in hostile lands outside of the pampering of Christian conferences.

What is the primary Holy Spirit experience in authentic Christian faith? The power to pick up the Cross in self-denial to be a witness for Jesus Christ. Not some kind of mystical high, and drunken state which pumps up the flesh. A cheap thrill, with no Cross, no blood, and confrontation. Not the work of the Holy Spirit.

John 16:7-15
7 Nevertheless I tell you the truth; It is expedient for you that I go away: for if I go not away, the Comforter will not come unto you; but if I depart, I will send him unto you.
8 And when he is come, he will reprove the world of sin, and of righteousness, and of judgment:
9 Of sin, because they believe not on me.
10 Of righteousness, because I go to my Father, and ye see me no more;
11 Of judgment, because the prince of this world is judged.
12 I have yet many things to say unto you, but ye cannot bear them now.
13 Howbeit when he, the Spirit of truth, is come, he will guide you into all truth: for he shall not speak of

himself; but whatsoever he shall hear, that shall he speak: and he will shew you things to come.

14 He shall glorify me: for he shall receive of mine, and shall shew it unto you.

15 All things that the Father hath are mine: therefore said I, that he shall take of mine, and shall shew it unto you

The Promise of the Father

The promise of the coming Holy Spirit given the original disciples before the Day of Pentecost was called the Promise of the Father.

Acts 1:1-5

The former treatise have I made, O Theophilus, of all that Jesus began both to do and teach,

2 Until the day in which he was taken up, after that he through the Holy Ghost had given commandments unto the apostles whom he had chosen:

3 To whom also he shewed himself alive after his passion by many infallible proofs, being seen of them forty days, and speaking of the things pertaining to the kingdom of God:

4 And, being assembled together with them, commanded them that they should not depart from Jerusalem, but wait for the promise of the Father, which, saith he, ye have heard of me. 5 For John truly baptized with water; but ye shall be baptized with the Holy Ghost not many days hence.

Notice the background these disciples had just seen Jesus Christ raised from the dead and were eyewitnesses to the Resurrection. If you think there was ever a time to tell the world what they had just seen and experienced, it was right now. However, Jesus Christ told them to wait as the need power to be a witness. Their promise was the coming Holy Spirit on the Day of Pentecost who would fill them with power to be a witness.

Being filled with the Holy Spirit is also called being Baptized in the Holy Spirit. The Scriptures set the boundaries of being Baptized with the Holy Spirit as an orthodox Christian experience. However, many doubt as to the continuance of the Baptism of the Holy Spirit with the Gifts of the Holy Spirit being for today. However, the apostle Peter has taught the Holy Spirit Baptism continues as long as God calls men and women into saving faith.

Acts 2:38-41
38 Then Peter said unto them, Repent, and be baptized every one of you in the name of Jesus Christ for the remission of sins, and ye shall receive the gift of the Holy Ghost.
39 For the promise is unto you, and to your children, and to all that are afar off, even as many as the LORD our God shall call.
40 And with many other words did he testify and exhort,

saying, Save yourselves from this untoward generation. ⁴¹ Then they that gladly received his word were baptized: and the same day there were added unto them about three thousand souls.

The continue of the Baptism of the Holy Spirit will continue until the Second Coming of Jesus Christ and the Gifts of the Holy Spirit are no longer needed. In the Book of Acts many years after the Day of Pentecost we see men and women newly Baptized in the Holy Spirit speaking in tongues and speaking prophetic words. Also, we see the apostles walking in the power of the Holy Spirit Baptism with many might miracles which drew large crowds to hear the preaching of the Gospel of Jesus Christ.

It is evident the first century Church continued in Pentecostal gifts speaking in tongues and manifesting all the gifts of the Holy Spirit. No first century Christians made light of the Baptism of the Holy Spirit even though many excess and errors were happening surround the practice of the gifts of the Holy Spirit.

With the Scriptures we have been given proper boundaries which define the gifts of the Holy Spirit their function and character. Keeping within the boundaries of the Scriptures will keep demonic counterfeit manifestations from being mistaken as the gifts of the Holy Spirit. Has tongues ceased, or should Christians preach against or forbid the speaking of tongues. The answer is found in the written Word of God which forbids Christians from stopping the function of the gifts of the Holy Spirit, including speaking in tongues or prophecy. However, tongues are to be in order only spoken in context according to Scriptures, and prophecy is to be judged according to the Scriptures.

One must not fear they will receive an evil spirit when seeking the gifts of the Holy Spirit. Keeping with the orthodoxy of Scriptures which define the charter of the nine gifts of the Holy Spirit and their proper use will allow every Christian to test the authenticity of any supernatural manifestation. For the manifestations of the gifts of the Holy Spirit are given to profit with all. Therefore, do not forbid to speak in tongues, and do not despise prophecy. However, all these gifts are to be done according to true function and order. For God is not the author of confusion but of peace.

The command of Scriptures is to be filled with the Holy Spirit, and to desire earnestly the gifts of the Holy Spirit. Despite all the controversy surrounding the Holy Spirit Baptism and Gifts of the Holy Spirit they are to be a major part of the Church practice and ministry. May God bless all those who hunger and thirst after God, and may they be filled with the Holy Spirit. Amen.

1 Corinthians 14:26-40

[26] How is it then, brethren? when ye come together, every one of you hath a psalm, hath a doctrine, hath a

tongue, hath a revelation, hath an interpretation. Let all things be done unto
edifying.

27 If any man speak in an unknown tongue, let it be by two, or at the most by three, and that by course; and let one interpret.

28 But if there be no interpreter, let him keep silence in the church; and let him speak to himself, and to God.

29 Let the prophets speak two or three and let the other judge.

30 If anything be revealed to another that sitteth by, let the first hold his peace.

31 For ye may all prophesy one by one, that all may learn, and all may be comforted.

32 And the spirits of the prophets are subject to the prophets.

33 For God is not the author of confusion, but of peace, as in all churches of the saints.

34 Let your women keep silence in the churches: for it is not permitted unto them to speak; but they are commanded to be under obedience as also saith the law.

35 And if they will learn anything, let them ask their husbands at home: for it is a shame for women to speak in the church.

36 What? came the word of God out from you? or came it unto you only?

37 If any man think himself to be a prophet, or spiritual, let him acknowledge that the things that I write unto you are the commandments of the Lord.

38 But if any man be ignorant, let him be ignorant.

39 Wherefore, brethren, covet to prophesy, and forbid not to speak with tongues.

40 Let all things be done decently and in order.

Power In the Blood

Don Pirozok

Gods Answer Is the Cross of Jesus Christ

The Sermon On the Mount

Jesus Christ Commands His Disciples

Don Pirozok

CHARISMATICS IN CRISIS

DON PIROZOK

Testing the Spirits of Prophets and Prophecy

Death Hell and Gods Curse

Don Pirozok